George and Marina

Christopher Warwick

George and Marina

Duke and Duchess of Kent

Weidenfeld and Nicolson · *London*

First published in Great Britain in 1988 by
George Weidenfeld & Nicolson Limited
91 Clapham High Street, London SW4 7TA

Printed and bound in Great Britain by The Bath Press, Avon

Dedicated to the memory of
my darling
TIMMI
15 December 1987

Beauty like hers is genius
(ROSSETTI)

Contents

Illustrations

(*Between pages 80 and 81*)

Prince George with his grandmother, Queen Alexandra (*BBC Hulton Picture Library*)

Prince John, Prince George and Prince Olav, 1910 (*Keystone*)

Princess Nicholas of Greece with her daughters (*Illustrated London News*)

The wedding of Prince George and Princess Marina, 1934 (*Bassano & Vandyk*)

Marina and George on honeymoon at Himley Hall (*Keystone*)

The Duchess of Kent receiving a bouquet of Alexandra roses (*Keystone*)

Noël Coward's informal snapshot of Princess Marina holding Alexandra (*Coward Archives*)

The Duke and Duchess of Kent attend a children's concert (*Keystone*)

Cecil Beaton's portrait of Princess Marina, 1938 (*by courtesy of the Trustees of the Victoria & Albert Museum*)

Princess Marina in a Greek-style dress (*Cecil Beaton, courtesy of the Trustees of the Victoria & Albert Museum*)

The Duchess in a suite of sapphires and diamonds (*Cecil Beaton, courtesy of the Trustees of the Victoria & Albert Museum*)

George and Marina's 1940 Christmas card (*Coward Archives*)

The Duke and Duchess visiting a hospital (*Keystone*)

Coppins in Iver, Buckinghamshire (*Tom Blau/Camera Press*)

The Duke and Duchess with Prince Michael, 1942 (*by courtesy of the Trustees of the Victoria & Albert Museum*)

The Duke with his elder son Eddie, 1942 *(by courtesy of the Trustees of the Victoria & Albert Museum)*

Princess Marina reading to Eddie and Alexandra *(by courtesy of the Trustees of the Victoria & Albert Museum)*

George and Marina at home, Coppins, 1942 *(by courtesy of the Trustees of the Victoria & Albert Museum)*

An aerial view of the crash site by Andrew Jack

The wreckage of the Sunderland *(After The Battle magazine)*

Prince George's coffin arrives at Euston *(Keystone)*

The Duchess as Commandant of the Wrens *(Keystone)*

Princess Marina and Eddie on a Far East tour, 1952 *(Keystone)*

Exchanging gifts with the Sultan of Brunei *(Camera Press)*

Noel Coward with Princess Marina and Princess Alexandra *(Camera Press)*

Presenting the women's championship trophy at Wimbledon, 1956 *(Keystone)*

The wedding of Edward, Duke of Kent and Katharine Worsley *(by courtesy of the Trustees of the Victoria & Albert Museum)*

After the wedding of Princess Alexandra and the Hon. Angus Ogilvy *(Associated Press)*

Princess Marina chatting to Princess Alice, 1967 *(Fox Photos)*

The funeral of Princess Marina, 1968 *(Times Newspapers Ltd)*

Princess Marina in the summer of 1964 *(Cecil Beaton/Camera Press)*

Acknowledgements

I should like to express my gratitude to a number of people whose contributions, whether great or small, have helped to make this book a reality. Some of those who gave of their time have asked not to be identified and, as in the past, I must respect that wish. To them, however, as to each of the following, I gladly extend my sincerest thanks:

The Lady Elizabeth Anson; Mrs Jean Auld; Mr Michael Bloch; Mr Frank S.FitzGerald-Bush; Mr John Cavanagh; the Lord Chamberlain's Office; Mr R.J.Evans; Mrs Valerie Garner; the reference section of the Greek Embassy; the India Office Library; Mme Kira Karageorgevitch (HSH Princess Kira zu Leiningen); Mr Robin Macwhirter; Miss Mona Mitchell, HRH Princess Juliana of the Netherlands; the Archivists of the Franklin D.Roosevelt Library, New York; Dr Jeremy Silver and Mr John Westmancoat of the National Sound Archives, London; the reference department of the United States Embassy; Mr Hugo Vickers; Mr Clifford Wade; Mrs Lily Wheeler; and Miss Audrey Whiting.

At the start of my research I had hoped that the Duke of Kent might respond favourably to a request for assistance. In the event, my approach was refused. However, Princess Alexandra did agree to reply to written questions.

Charlotte Balazs, who acted as my research assistant, deserves a page of thanks all to herself, as indeed, does Brian Auld, who once again acted as my chief sounding-board.

Lastly, I would like to offer my warmest thanks to Alex MacCormick of Weidenfeld & Nicolson for having invited me to undertake this biography. I can only hope her confidence has been justified.

Christopher Warwick

British Royal Family

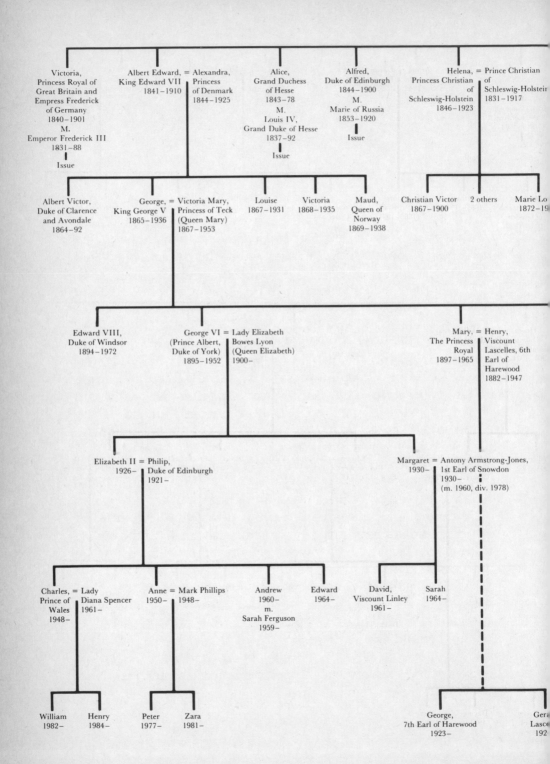

Victoria,
Princess Royal of
Great Britain and
Empress Frederick
of Germany
1840–1901
M.
Emperor Frederick III
1831–88

Issue

Albert Edward, = Alexandra,
King Edward VII   Princess
1841–1910   of Denmark
                 1844–1925

Alice,
Grand Duchess
of Hesse
1843–78
M.
Louis IV,
Grand Duke of Hesse
1837–92

Issue

Alfred,
Duke of Edinburgh
1844–1900
M.
Marie of Russia
1853–1920

Issue

Helena, = Prince Christian
Princess Christian   of
of   Schleswig-Holstein
Schleswig-Holstein   1831–1917
1846–1923

Albert Victor,
Duke of Clarence
and Avondale
1864–92

George, = Victoria Mary,
King George V   Princess of Teck
1865–1936   (Queen Mary)
                1867–1953

Louise
1867–1931

Victoria
1868–1935

Maud,
Queen of
Norway
1869–1938

Christian Victor
1867–1900

2 others

Marie Lo
1872–19

Edward VIII,
Duke of Windsor
1894–1972

George VI = Lady Elizabeth
(Prince Albert,   Bowes Lyon
Duke of York)   (Queen Elizabeth)
1895–1952   1900–

Mary, = Henry,
The Princess   Viscount
Royal   Lascelles, 6th
1897–1965   Earl of
               Harewood
               1882–1947

Elizabeth II = Philip,
1926–   Duke of Edinburgh
               1921–

Margaret = Antony Armstrong-Jones,
1930–   1st Earl of Snowdon
           1930–
           (m. 1960, div. 1978)

Charles, = Lady
Prince of   Diana Spencer
Wales   1961–
1948–

Anne = Mark Phillips
1950–   1948–

Andrew
1960–
m.
Sarah Ferguson
1959–

Edward
1964–

David,
Viscount Linley
1961–

Sarah
1964–

William
1982–

Henry
1984–

Peter
1977–

Zara
1981–

George,
7th Earl of Harewood
1923–

Gera
Lasce
192

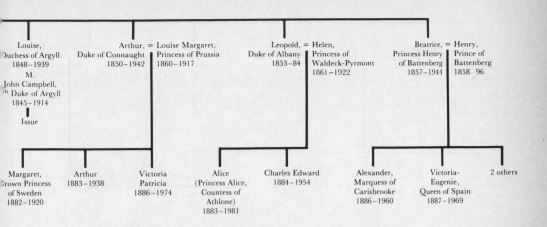

Louise,
Duchess of Argyll
1848–1939
M.
John Campbell,
th Duke of Argyll
1845–1914

Issue

Arthur, = Louise Margaret,
Duke of Connaught | Princess of Prussia
1850–1942 | 1860–1917

Leopold, = Helen,
Duke of Albany | Princess of
1853–84 | Waldeck-Pyrmont
| 1861–1922

Beatrice, = Henry,
Princess Henry | Prince of
of Battenberg | Battenberg
1857–1944 | 1858 96

Margaret,
Crown Princess
of Sweden
1882–1920

Arthur
1883–1938

Victoria
Patricia
1886–1974

Alice
(Princess Alice,
Countess of
Athlone)
1883–1981

Charles Edward
1884–1954

Alexander,
Marquess of
Carisbrooke
1886–1960

Victoria-
Eugenie,
Queen of Spain
1887–1969

2 others

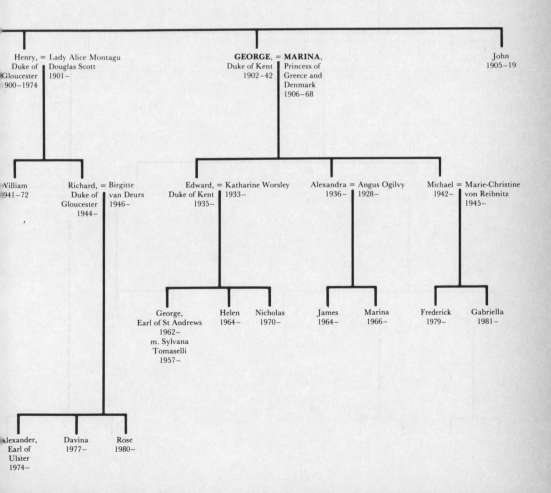

Henry, = Lady Alice Montagu
Duke of | Douglas Scott
Gloucester | 1901–
900–1974

GEORGE, = MARINA,
Duke of Kent | Princess of
1902–42 | Greece and
| Denmark
| 1906–68

John
1905–19

William
941–72

Richard, = Birgitte
Duke of | van Deurs
Gloucester | 1946–
1944–

Edward, = Katharine Worsley
Duke of Kent | 1933–
1935–

Alexandra = Angus Ogilvy
1936– | 1928–

Michael = Marie-Christine
1942– | von Reibnitz
| 1945–

George,
Earl of St Andrews
1962–
m. Sylvana
Tomaselli
1957–

Helen
1964–

Nicholas
1970–

James
1964–

Marina
1966–

Frederick
1979–

Gabriella
1981–

Alexander,
Earl of
Ulster
1974–

Davina
1977–

Rose
1980–

Russian and Greek Royal Families

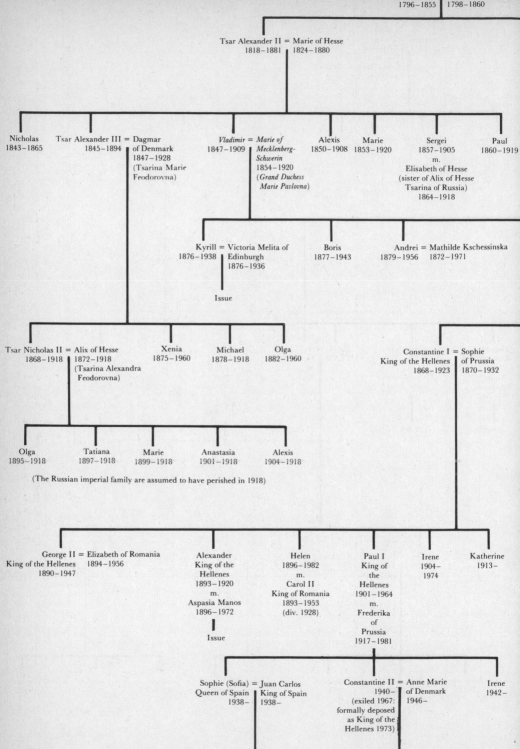

Nicholas I = Charlotte
Tsar of Russia | of Prussia
1796–1855 | 1798–1860

Tsar Alexander II = Marie of Hesse
1818–1881 | 1824–1880

Nicholas 1843–1865

Tsar Alexander III = Dagmar of Denmark 1845–1894 | 1847–1928 (Tsarina Marie Feodorovna)

Vladimir = *Marie of* 1847–1909 | *Mecklenberg-Schwerin* 1854–1920 (*Grand Duchess Marie Pavlovna*)

Alexis 1850–1908

Marie 1853–1920

Sergei 1857–1905 m. Elisabeth of Hesse (sister of Alix of Hesse Tsarina of Russia) 1864–1918

Paul 1860–1919

Kyrill = Victoria Melita of 1876–1938 | Edinburgh 1876–1936

Issue

Boris 1877–1943

Andrei = Mathilde Kschessinska 1879–1956 | 1872–1971

Tsar Nicholas II = Alix of Hesse 1868–1918 | 1872–1918 (Tsarina Alexandra Feodorovna)

Xenia 1875–1960

Michael 1878–1918

Olga 1882–1960

Constantine I = Sophie King of the Hellenes | of Prussia 1868–1923 | 1870–1932

Olga 1895–1918

Tatiana 1897–1918

Marie 1899–1918

Anastasia 1901–1918

Alexis 1904–1918

(The Russian imperial family are assumed to have perished in 1918)

George II = Elizabeth of Romania King of the Hellenes | 1894–1956 1890–1947

Alexander King of the Hellenes 1893–1920 m. Aspasia Manos 1896–1972

Issue

Helen 1896–1982 m. Carol II King of Romania 1893–1953 (div. 1928)

Paul I King of the Hellenes 1901–1964 m. Frederika of Prussia 1917–1981

Irene 1904–1974

Katherine 1913–

Sophie (Sofia) = Juan Carlos Queen of Spain | King of Spain 1938– | 1938–

Issue

Constantine II = Anne Marie 1940– | of Denmark (exiled 1967: | 1946– formally deposed as King of the Hellenes 1973)

Issue

Irene 1942–

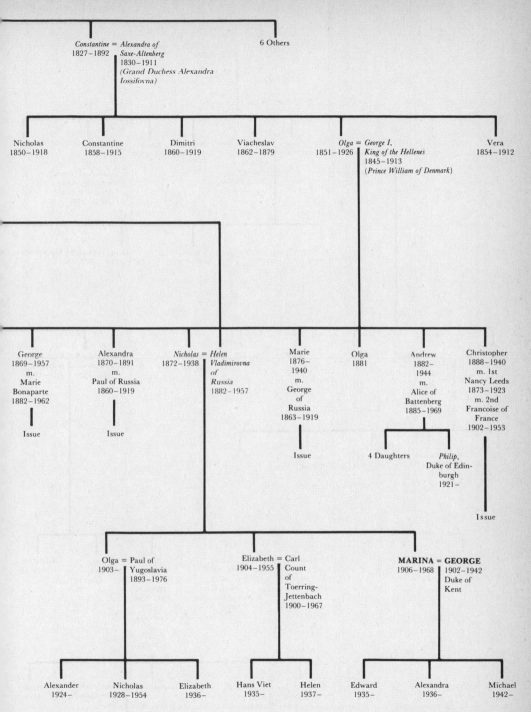

Constantine = Alexandra of
1827–1892   Saxe-Altenberg
            1830–1911
            *(Grand Duchess Alexandra
            Iossifovna)*

6 Others

Nicholas   Constantine   Dimitri   Viacheslav   Olga = George I,   Vera
1850–1918   1858–1915   1860–1919 1862–1879   1851–1926 King of the Hellenes 1854–1912
                                                              1845–1913
                                                              (Prince William of Denmark)

George   Alexandra   *Nicholas = Helen*   Marie   Olga   Andrew   Christopher
1869–1957   1870–1891   *1872–1938 Vladimirovna*   1876–   1881   1882–   1888–1940
m.   m.   *of*   1940   1944   m. 1st
Marie   Paul of Russia   *Russia*   m.   m.   Nancy Leeds
Bonaparte   1860–1919   *1882–1957*   George   Alice of   1873–1923
1882–1962   of   Battenberg   m. 2nd
                                                     Russia   1885–1969   Francoise of
                                                     1863–1919   France
                                                                                   1902–1953

Issue   Issue   4 Daughters   *Philip,*
                                                     Issue   Duke of Edin-
                                                                                  burgh
                                                                                  1921–

                                                                                              Issue

            Olga = Paul of   Elizabeth = Carl   **MARINA = GEORGE**
            1903– Yugoslavia   1904–1955 Count   1906–1968 1902–1942
                   1893–1976   of   Duke of
                                                Toerring-   Kent
                                                Jettenbach
                                                1900–1967

Alexander   Nicholas   Elizabeth   Hans Viet   Helen   Edward   Alexandra   Michael
1924–   1928–1954   1936–   1935–   1937–   1935–   1936–   1942–

                                                             (see British royal family tree)

Foreword

Prince George and Princess Marina, Duke and Duchess of Kent, were regarded as the most attractive, popular and, above all, stylish royal couple of their generation. As such they are still remembered to this day.

Until the time of his marriage in 1934, Prince George, the youngest surviving son of King George v and Queen Mary, was seen very much as a 'high flyer'. Impetuous and reckless, he chose a way of life that caused as much consternation within his family during the 1920s and 30s as his memory does today. That the royal family has never allowed an official biography of him bears eloquent testimony to that fact.

With an assortment of friends, some illustrious, others more shady, and an outer and much wider circle of admirers and acquaintances eager for his favours, George brought a vivid flash of colour into the largely colourless environs of the Royal House of Windsor.

Artistic, good looking, intelligent and immensely sociable, Prince George, who always possessed 'a clear tinge of narcissism', developed a taste for adventure that proved disconcerting. A former royal equerry was to say that, as a young man, George was always 'in trouble', adding spice to his remark by revealing that so many of the Prince's associates were chased out of the country 'that the Palace stopped counting'.

At the age of thirty-two George finally married, and though his reputation as a playboy was to outlive him, the tone of his life, and the speed at which he lived it, were tempered by a greater sense of responsibility. At thirty-nine, however, he was dead; the victim of an air disaster which, almost half a century later, remains shrouded in mystery.

The woman Prince George married was certainly no less artistic, good-looking or intelligent. She was Princess Marina of Greece and Denmark. As Duke and Duchess of Kent – 'that dazzling pair' as they were once described – George and Marina dominated London society, gathering around them some of the most brilliant personalities from the world of the arts, entertaining lavishly and generating an interest in their way of life that was unparalleled in the history of the British royal family.

When she came to England at the time of her marriage, Marina was unknown to the public; an obscure foreign princess who had spent the past twelve years of her life in exile. On the day she stepped ashore at Folkestone in 1934, that obscurity vanished for ever. Here, as the crowds waiting to catch a glimpse of her were quick to recognize, was no commonplace princess. The people's spontaneous response that day ultimately determined the way in which Marina would be regarded throughout her life in Britain.

If anything, the Duke of Kent's sudden death in 1942, only eight years after they were married, served to enhance Marina's appeal still further. Yet the subsequent image of her as a tragic widow devoted entirely to good works and raising her three children paints less than half of a much more colourful picture. Princess Marina was always a resourceful woman with a zest for life and the means and ability to enjoy it. Widowhood did nothing to alter that.

The life of Princess Marina, Duchess of Kent, was destined to be comparatively short. She died on 27 August 1968 at the age of sixty-one. Since then there has been but one biography of Marina herself, and none of Prince George. The aim of this study, therefore, is not only to recall the story of one of this century's most popular royal figures on the twentieth anniversary of her death, but also to paint a portrait of a partnership that fascinated the world.

Chapter One

Imperial Heritage

Tsarskoe Selo, for two hundred years the summer retreat of the tsars of Russia, lies some fifteen miles south of Leningrad, on land stretching back from the Gulf of Finland. Here in 1718 the Empress Catherine, wife of Tsar Peter I, had had built a modest stone house. Less than forty years later, under the direction of the Empress Elizabeth, that earlier structure had given way to a palace of monumental proportions.

The Great Catherine – or Yekaterininsky – Palace was the work of the Italian architect Bartolomeo Francesco Rastrelli. Responsible for building a number of palaces in and around Leningrad, or St Petersburg as it was then known, Rastrelli embodied in the palace every extravagant mood and nuance of the Baroque school. One façade, washed a subtle blue-green and ornamented with rows of towering columns, ornate window surrounds and wrought-iron balconies, stretched for a thousand yards. At the southern end, a single golden dome rose majestically over the Grand Staircase, while at the northern end, five more domes – each heavily gilded with solid gold leaf – rose in a cluster above the church which the Empress Elizabeth had incorporated into the palace itself.

It was in this church, where religious paintings were set like decorative panels into royal blue walls, and where pillars heavy with gilded vines supported golden angels, that the story of Princess Marina, Duchess of Kent, may be said to have its roots. For it was here, in a long and solemn ritual – the origins of which were nearly as old as time itself – that her parents were married on 29 August 1902.

Princess Marina's father, Prince Nicholas of Greece, born on

27 January 1872, was the third son and fourth child of King George
I and Queen Olga of the Hellenes. Nicholas was the grandson
of King Christian IX and Queen Louise of Denmark, and the
nephew of both Britain's Queen Alexandra, consort of King
Edward VII, and her younger sister Dagmar who, as the Tsarina
Marie Feodorovna, consort of Tsar Alexander III, would be Russia's penultimate empress.

Prince Nicholas's bride on that summer's day long ago was the
Grand Duchess Helen Vladimirovna, only daughter of the Grand
Duke Vladimir and his German-born wife, Princess Marie of Meck-
lenberg-Schwerin, granddaughter of the murdered Tsar-Liberator
Alexander II, niece of Tsar Alexander III, and first cousin of the
ill-fated Tsar Nicholas II, last of Russia's imperial masters. Born
on 17 January 1882, a decade almost to the very day after the
birth of her husband, the Grand Duchess Helen was, to quote
Prince Nicholas, 'lovely and fascinating'. Indeed the Prince described himself as 'the proud winner of a lovely bride who had
won for herself a place in all hearts by her sweet nature and unself-
ishness'.

The marriage of Prince and Princess Nicholas of Greece, provided one more link in an immensely intricate chain: a chain that
connected the Russian imperial house of Romanov with the intimate network of royal families that, until the end of the Great
War, dominated Europe's political and social structure. Of his
immediate family, Prince Nicholas followed not only the example
of his sisters Alexandra and Marie in marrying a Romanov but,
more notably, that of his father, King George I of Greece. More-
over, if in 1902, as he claimed in his memoirs, Prince Nicholas
felt 'conscience-stricken' at taking his wife away from her family,
to say nothing of the splendour of her life in St Petersburg and
at Tsarskoe Selo, then his emotions undoubtedly echoed those
of the young King George little more than thirty years earlier.

The Greek monarchy was, compared to that of Russia, of relatively recent origin, dating back only to 1832 with the accession
of Prince Otto of Bavaria to the throne of a newly independent
Greece. His despotic rule was to provoke two revolutions. King
George I of the Hellenes was born Prince William of Denmark
on Christmas Eve 1845. In 1863, at the age of eighteen, he found
himself elected to the vacant throne of Greece after Otto's final
deposition. Four years later he took himself off to Russia in search

of a wife. His immediate choice was the sixteen-year-old Grand Duchess Olga Constantinovna, eldest daughter of the massively rich Grand Duke Constantine and Princess Alexandra of Saxe-Altenburg, Duchess of Saxony. The marriage of King George and the young Grand Duchess was celebrated at the Winter Palace in St Petersburg on 15 October 1867. Within days the new Queen of Greece, whose youth and immaturity were emphasized by the trunk full of dolls included in her luggage, was *en route* to a new country and a new people. In time the King's child bride would become one of the best-loved queens in the turbulent history of the Greek monarchy, while she in turn would develop an abiding affection for the volatile nation over which her husband had been chosen to rule. Yet throughout a long and eventful life, which included raising a family of five sons and two daughters,* Queen Olga always felt homesick, pining, especially during the early years, not just for the company of her own family but for Russia itself. Indeed, it has been said that leaving the land of her birth imbued the Queen with a profound and permanent sense of loss.

Fortunately for the 'conscience' of King George and Queen Olga's son Nicholas, the twenty-year-old Grand Duchess Helen did not experience similar emotions when she married and surrendered the security of her homeland for the simpler, infinitely more primitive way of life in Greece. But like her mother-in-law before her, the young Princess Nicholas could not avoid discovering some of the more obvious disadvantages of life in Athens. For example, the royal palace where she and her husband spent the first three years of their married life was old-fashioned, uncomfortable and draughty; a house in which only two bathrooms served more than 300 rooms, and where cockroaches were more likely to spill from the bath taps than water.

By contrast, the discomfort Prince and Princess Nicholas endured at the royal palace was alleviated by the regular visits they made to Tatoi, King George's 40,000-acre estate thirty miles or so outside Athens. Situated in densely wooded grounds at the foot of the Párnis in the Plain of Attica, and surrounded by plane trees, acacias, cypresses, poplars and pines, Tatoi was to the Greek

---

* Constantine, afterwards King Constantine I, 1868–1923; George, 1869–1957; Alexandra, 1870–1891; Nicholas, 1872–1938; Marie, 1876–1940; Andrew, 1882–1944; Christopher, 1888–1940. A third daughter, Olga, was born and died in 1880.

royal family what Balmoral or Sandringham were – and still are – to their British relations: a private family hideaway.

Prince Nicholas wrote in his autobiography, published in 1926:

> Of all the places where I have lived, either in Greece or any other country, Tatoi will always stand out as the dwelling round which are centred the happiest recollections of my life as a child and as a man. For my parents, as well as for us children, Tatoi represented our real home – the place that belonged to us, where everyone was free to do as he liked. For my parents it meant a rest in their life devoted to its many duties. . . . For us it represented liberty, independence, the scene of our wildest romps and frolics.

It was at Tatoi on 11 June 1903, shortly before her first wedding anniversary, that Princess Nicholas gave birth to the eldest of her three daughters, who was baptized Olga in tribute to her paternal grandmother. Her sister Elizabeth was born eleven months later, on 24 May 1904. Yet if all had gone well for Princess Nicholas over the arrival of her first two children, the birth of the youngest, Marina, was to give rise to considerable alarm. For whatever reason, and it has never been explained sufficiently clearly, Princess Nicholas's third and last confinement on 13 December 1906 – or 30 November, according to the old-style Greek calendar – proved to be a particularly harrowing experience, as much for the anguished father as for the mother herself. Even in his memoirs Prince Nicholas chose to reveal little about the circumstances surrounding his youngest daughter's birth. All he disclosed was that, after Marina's delivery, Princess Nicholas had been 'so seriously ill' that he 'lived through moments of terrible anguish'. For a long time, the Prince wrote, his wife had been 'so fragile that she could take little or no part in public life', adding that for two years running the Princess had undertaken 'a treatment' at the famous health spa at Franzensbad. Many years later, Prince Nicholas was to say of his youngest and, some claim, his favourite daughter, 'She was a very dear baby. She nearly cost her mother her life.'

Unlike her sisters, Princess Marina – who was named at the suggestion of her grandfather King George I after 'one of the best loved of all Greek saints' – was born not at Tatoi, but at the newly completed Nicholas Palace in Athens, where her parents had taken up residence late in 1905. This imposing whitewashed house – more mansion than palace – had been built for Prince and Princess Nicholas as a wedding present from Tsar Alexander III. Filled with treasures collected by the discerning Prince, shaded by fig trees and set in a garden brimming with oleander and bougainvillea, the Nicholas Palace was the very height of modernity – and the envy of all. Situated on a wide boulevard that was later named the Avenue Queen Sophie, in honour of the wife of Marina's uncle 'Tino', later King Constantine I of Greece, the palace was not only considered to be the most elegant edifice of its kind in all Athens, but contained such luxuries as central heating, hot and cold running water, and several bathrooms, each fitted with heated towel rails.

Until revolution scattered the Greek royal family in 1917, life for Prince Nicholas, his wife and daughters was as close to perfection as it is possible to get. And while they were happy to lead comparatively simple lives at the most democratic, least ceremonious court in Europe, they lacked few of the material comforts and privileges accorded to royalty the world over.

If in retrospect, therefore, Princess Marina's childhood seemed bathed in perpetual sunlight, as some have since claimed, later events in her life would inevitably assume less blissful characteristics. 'She is a child of destiny, and there is both sunshine and shadow for her,' a gypsy woman foretold when Marina was but a few months old. 'She will be beautiful and make a great marriage with a king's son. Love will be her guiding star. It will bring her sorrow, for she will lose her husband while she is still young and at the height of her happiness. But she will find consolation in her children.'

Though Princess Nicholas was devoted to each of her daughters, her idea of motherhood stopped short at breastfeeding. That task, according to custom, was entrusted to local peasant women engaged as wetnurses. Once the children were weaned, their welfare was the responsibility of their redoubtable, Norland-trained nanny, Miss Kate Fox. She spoon-fed them camomile tea, sponged their bodies with cold sea water, encouraged physical exercise and, as her three charges reached the toddler stage, allowed them to play virtually naked in the garden of their home. "My poor father was in despair and predicted that their complexions would be ruined forever when he saw these children become as brown as berries,' Prince Nicholas later recalled. But English practices insisted on by a typically English nanny won the whole-hearted support of Prince and Princess Nicholas, both champions of the English way of life, despite the anxious protests of both sets of grandparents, used to swaddling their offspring in unnecessary layers of clothing, and allowing them out into the sunshine only if suitably attired and protected by parasols and lace-trimmed bonnets, or both.

Radical though Miss Fox's methods of raising children may have seemed to some, their practical benefits were always much in evidence during the development of Princess Marina and her elder sisters. It was also due partly to the efforts of 'Foxy', as she was known to the family, that an operation in 1911 to straighten Marina's left foot proved such a success. At birth it had been discovered that her left leg was not only thinner and fractionally shorter than the right, but that her left foot had been twisted to one side. Some have even asserted that it was badly misshapen as a result. Be that as it may, Foxy massaged the Princess's foot twice daily for five years. The eventual operation achieved its main objective, though of course little or nothing could be done to improve the condition of the weak leg itself. The long-term effect was that Princess Marina always wore shoes that were specially designed to correct the almost imperceptible imbalance. Throughout her life Marina coped admirably with this minor deformity. As a child she was never known to allow it to impede her games or, for that matter, some of the more strenuous pursuits – swimming, tennis or riding – that she shared with her sisters and their close circle of girl cousins.

Jennifer Ellis, one of Marina's earliest biographers, wrote:

> Like all strong-willed, lively children, she was often in conflict with authority. She had . . . tremendous force of character. It made her the leader among her sisters and cousins*. . . . In her determination not to be left out of

---

* All princesses, Marina's girl cousins were: Helen, later Queen of Romania; Irene and Katherine, daughters of Prince Nicholas's elder brother, Constantine, Duke of Sparta, afterwards King Constantine I of Greece; and Margarita, Theodora, Cecile and Sophie, sisters of Prince Philip, Duke of Edinburgh, and daughters of Prince Nicholas's younger brother, Andrew.

anything, she had to take life at a tremendous pace, always trying to catch up with the others, and usually succeeding through sheer will-power. She learnt to swim at three by hurling [herself] into the swimming pool in imitation of Olga's dive. She learnt to ride by galloping off on a horse far too big for her in pursuit of Elizabeth . . . . She had an invincible courage for any adventure.

Informal though the lives of Princess Marina and her siblings may have been, their daily routine, albeit devoid of any rigid etiquette, was always strictly adhered to, for, as Prince Nicholas once explained to Foxy, "I want my children to be brought up in an atmosphere of love. But whilst I do not wish them to be thwarted, I do not want them to be spoiled.' To all intents and purposes Prince Nicholas had his way. Yet it is impossible to believe that, as the youngest member of an extremely close and united family, Marina was not the object of special attention, fussed over and indulged. In later years even Prince Nicholas had to admit that his youngest daughter could 'always get away with anything', often with a cheeky retort. Admonished for some misdeed, Marina was told by her father that she must tell God she was sorry. 'What would be the use?' she asked. 'If God knows everything He must know I'm sorry without being told.' On another occasion, when trying to coax the young Princess – who was never keen on her music lessons – into practising the piano, Prince Nicholas sat down at the keyboard and picked out a tune with one finger.

'Come along', he cajoled, 'you see Papa trying, don't you?'

'Yes', Marina answered, 'that's why I don't.'

Even when it came to saying her evening prayers, the Princess knew best. Asked by her grandmother, Queen Olga, why she did not pray in Greek, she replied, 'I've arranged it with God. I told Him I liked to talk to Him in English best, and He said, "Please yourself, Marina. All languages are the same to me."'

To many observers of royal lives, and it is particularly true of the more sentimental biographers, signs of precocity in royal children have invariably been excused in the most unctuous terms. Wilful or arrogant behaviour has been put down to natural high spirits or explained, though unconvincingly, as evidence of character or intelligence. In this instance many stories related of the young Princess Marina tend to suggest that, far from being any kind of paragon, she was, quite simply, a precocious child who, as she matured, became one of the most strong-minded and determined of women.

Chapter Two

Russian Twilight

Marina was already seven by the time her formal education began. Joining her sisters Olga and Elizabeth in their white-walled schoolroom with its view of the Acropolis, she was taught by three governesses. Yet while she learned quickly, especially in subjects that fired her imagination such as literature, geography and art, she lacked concentration in other studies, among them music – even though she was to adore it as an adult – mathematics, which always defeated her, and to some extent history. 'You know all the names of the cinema stars,' Prince Nicholas once reproached her, 'but you don't seem to take the trouble to remember the names of the Kings of England.' Whatever her deficiencies in some subjects, however, Marina more than made up for them in others. Her aptitude for languages meant that, apart from Greek and English, in which she had been schooled from birth, she became fluent in French, German, Italian and Russian.

In art she also excelled, demonstrating considerable skill in portraiture, landscape and still life. In this area her talents strongly resembled those of her father, an accomplished painter in his own right. As a toddler Marina often wandered into his studio to watch him work or to dip her fingers into his paints in an attempt to assist him. Later on father and daughter would take themselves off, set up their easels and spend long summer afternoons painting side by side. Together they became students of Byzantine religious art and, intrigued by any news they might hear of new archaeological discoveries, frequently accompanied one another to the sites of current excavations.

If interests such as these bound Prince Nicholas and his youngest daughter still further, they also shared another great love in common, that of the theatre. Without doubt the cultured and erudite Prince Nicholas was Greece's foremost royal patron of the arts. A poet, a writer and a lover and collector of books, paintings and *objets d'art*, he was also in the privileged position of being able to indulge his passion for drama in the most creative way possible. Not only did he write and produce a large number of plays and often act in them as well but he was also able to do so in his very own theatre. It was on the stage of the 'Royal Theatre' in Athens, as it was known, that the young Princess Marina appeared in prominent roles, from *tableaux vivants* devised by her father and based on scenes from Greek mythology, to Shakespeare's *The Merchant of Venice* and Corneille's *Le Cid*. Amateur actors such as Princess Marina, her sisters and cousins were not alone in treading the boards of Prince Nicholas's theatre, however. On many occasions the royal troupe made way for infinitely more august thespians, such as the legendary Sarah Bernhardt herself.

Varied though Marina's life in Athens was, she and her family were at their most content at Tatoi. Among the Princess's childhood memories, some of the most vivid were the haunting roar of stags issuing from the forest at night; the occasional glimpse of wolves silhouetted against a winter sky; the animals of Tatoi's home farm, where every creature was given a pet name, and summer picnics on the beach at Phaleron. Nor did time dim the Princess's memories of outings to local villages, where residents in national costume rushed towards the royal carriages bearing gifts of flowers or embroidery, or of her visits to Spetsai. Though she was never able to explain why, this of all the Greek islands forever remained Marina's favourite.

Foreign travel also became a prominent feature of the Princess's life. To begin with, of course, journeys took the form of holidays, either with her parents and sisters or with Foxy acting as nurse and guardian. Perhaps Marina's earliest journey abroad was that which took place in about 1908, when she, Olga and Elizabeth were taken to Finland to stay with an intimate friend of Princess Nicholas at her house on the shores of the Gulf. A little later, in 1910, Marina was taken to England for the first time. It was then, at the age of three and a half, that she was entertained to tea at Buckingham Palace, and introduced to King George v and Queen Mary who, almost a quarter of a century later, would become her parents-in-law.

In 1910, the year of her husband's accession to the throne, Queen Mary's interest in Marina extended no further than that of a godmother meeting her goddaughter for the first time. During that holiday Prince and Princess Nicholas also took their daughters to Sandringham in Norfolk to visit their great-aunt, the recently widowed Queen Alexandra. Described as Britain's most beautiful queen, 'Aunt Alix', as Prince Nicholas always knew her, had come to Britain from Denmark early in 1863 as the bride of the future Edward VII, whose death she now mourned. Incidentally, when Princess Marina came to England in 1934 as the fiancée of Prince George, Duke of Kent, her close resemblance to the esteemed Queen Alexandra – who had died in November 1925 – was widely remarked upon.

From Sandringham, during that first visit, Marina and her sisters were taken to Bognor. Foxy later recalled:

> Their parents came to see them settled in there, and then HRH Princess Victoria [daughter of Edward VII and Queen Alexandra] stayed for some time at the Norfolk Hotel, when she saw a lot of the three little girls, who helped her to bear the sad loss in the death of King Edward, whom, unhappily, Princess Marina never saw.
>
> At Bognor the Princess and her sisters had a very happy time, and, like less exalted children, busied themselves in making castles and all sorts of fine things in the sand. They were often helped by Princess Victoria and by their uncle, Prince Christopher of Greece [youngest brother of Prince Nicholas], who spent some time there.

Holidays in more exotic locations were soon to follow, but until the Revolution in 1917, none could surpass the excitement of family visits to Princess Nicholas's home in Russia. St Petersburg, conceived by Peter the Great in 1712 as the new capital city of an empire that covered one-sixth of the world's land surface and contained 130 million people, was built on a marshy archipelago at the head of the Baltic Sea. The construction of this magnificent city – spanning nineteen islands linked one to the other by elegant bridges and interwoven with winding canals – claimed the lives of no fewer than 200,000 labourers. Through the centre of St Petersburg, called the 'Venice of the North' or the 'Babylon of the Snows', flowed the River Neva, on the south bank of which were built the Winter Palace, official residence of the tsars, several embassies and the palaces of the nobility. One of them, known as the Marble Palace (now the Lenin Museum) belonged to Prince Nicholas's maternal grandparents, the Grand Duke Constantine and the Grand Duchess Alexandra Iossifovna. Another, the equally splendid Vladimir Palace, situated close to the Hermitage, had been built for Princess Nicholas's parents, the Grand Duke and Grand Duchess Vladimir. Perhaps better known as the Grand Duchess Marie Pavlovna, this German-born princess was considered to be more Russian than the Russians, so profound was her love for her adopted country. Indeed, throughout her married life, and even after the death of her husband in 1909, the formidable Grand Duchess Vladimir, who ranked after the Empress Alexandra and the Dowager Empress Marie Feodorovna as the third lady in the land, was the acknowledged doyenne of Russian society. Princess Marina's cultured and powerful grandparents held the most glittering court in the entire empire. The brilliance of its ceremonial, together with the fame, accomplishments and position of all who flocked to it, never failed to eclipse the court of Tsar Nicholas II himself.

Partly as a result of this, relations between the Vladimirs and the Tsar and Tsarina were never harmonious. At best they were precariously balanced. Nicholas II, not only a weak man but also an ineffectual ruler, was too easily dominated by his wife Alexandra. The once attractive Princess Alix of Hesse-Darmstadt, favourite granddaughter of Queen Victoria, became almost insanely neurotic due to constant fear for the life of her haemophiliac son, the Tsarevitch Alexis. Henpecked by a superstitious wife – who clung desperately to the sinister moujik Rasputin, whose hypnotic powers 'miraculously' saved the Tsarevitch from bleeding to death on many occasions – Nicholas II was just as easily intimidated by his forceful uncles. The eldest, Grand Duke Vladimir, said to have been one of Russia's most brilliant historians, held office both as Commander of the Imperial Guard and Commander of the St Petersburg Garrison, which in effect meant that he was commander-in-chief of the entire Russian Army. As such he had enormous influence over the Tsar, as did his brothers, the Grand Dukes Alexis and Sergei, respectively Grand Admiral of the Russian Navy and Governor-General of Moscow. The Tsar, according to his cousin the Grand Duke Alexander,

... dreaded to be left alone with them. In the presence of witnesses his opinions were accepted as orders, but the instant the door of his study closed on the outsider, down on the table would go with a bang the weighty fist of Uncle Alexis. ... Uncle Serge and Uncle Vladimir developed equally efficient methods of intimidation .... They all had their favourite generals and admirals ... their wonderful preachers anxious to redeem the Emperor's soul ... their clairvoyant peasants with a divine message.

Nor was intrigue and rancour the exclusive preserve of the Tsar's uncles alone. So vehemently opposed to the Empress's interference in the government of the country was the Grand Duchess Vladimir that as late as January 1917 she hatched a dramatic, if ultimately futile, plot of her own. With Russian troops being lost in their tens of thousands in the Great War, and carefully engineered sedition encouraging discontent in the cities, the Grand Duchess invited Michael Rodzianko, President of the Duma [Parliament] to lunch with her at the Vladimir Palace. Of their meeting, Rodzianko later wrote that the Grand Duchess

... began to talk of the general state of affairs, of the Government's incompetence, of Protopopov [Alexander Protopopov, Minister of the Interior, responsible for the preservation of law and order], and of the Empress. She mentioned the latter's name, becoming more and more excited, dwelling on her nefarious influence and interference in everything, and said she was driving the country to destruction ....

Something, said the Grand Duchess, must be done. Somebody must be removed, destroyed.

'What do you mean by "removed"?' Rodzianko asked.

'The Duma must do something. She must be annihilated,' the Grand Duchess replied. When asked to whom she referred, Marie Pavlovna answered, 'The Empress.' Startled, her guest insisted that he be allowed to treat their conversation as though it had never taken place, 'because if you address me as the President of the Duma, my oath of allegiance compels me to wait at once on His Imperial Majesty and report to him that the Grand Duchess

Marie Pavlovna has declared to me that the Empress must be annihilated'.

Nothing came of the Grand Duchess Vladimir's schemes, of course, even though news of her plans for four regiments of the Guard to seize the Tsar and Tsarina in a night-time raid on Tsarskoe Selo, followed by the enforced abdication of Nicholas II and the establishment of a regency under the Tsar's distant cousin, the Grand Duke Nicholas Nicolaievich, was circulated for society's amusement. Two months later, on 15 March 1917, Tsar Nicholas II did abdicate, though that event and all that followed reached far beyond anything the Grand Duchess Vladimir could have imagined.

Though she was far too young to have realized it, the Russia of Princess Marina's childhood was still firmly entrenched in its tyrannical past; a country alarmingly medieval in its contrasts between splendour and squalor, feudal in its relations between nobility and peasantry. While the rich pampered themselves in spectacular fashion, the poor – in other words, three-quarters of the entire population – toiled, starved and died in abject poverty. The last time Princess Marina ever visited Russia was during the summer of 1914, shortly before her eighth birthday. Less than three years later revolution would engulf the empire, crushing the 300-year-old Romanov autocracy for ever.

Marina's personal memories of the holidays she spent at her grandmother's palaces in St Petersburg and Tsarskoe Selo were comparatively few. Later on, images of people, places and events were sketched in for her, if not by family reminiscences, then by the lessons of history itself. Among her most distinct memories, however, were the annual journeys she made aboard the imperial train with her parents and sisters. Put at their disposal to ferry them from Sebastopol to St Petersburg every summer – and at the beginning and end of occasional winter visits as well – the train consisted of several carriages, each furnished to afford royal passengers the greatest possible comfort. The day saloons were upholstered in rich fabrics, the floors laid with thick carpeting, while the sleeping quarters were equipped with proper beds covered with fine linens and eiderdowns of pure silk.

Far greater opulence awaited Princess Nicholas and her family once the long, slow, journey to her mother's official residence had been completed. Indeed, it would have been surprising if, as an adult, Princess Marina had not been able to recall something of the magnificence of her grandmother's homes. The Vladimir Palace, Florentine in concept and impressively built of brown stone, was lavishly furnished with antiques in the style of the eighteenth century. The walls of the Grand Duchess Marie Pavlovna's salons were hung with Gobelin tapestries, paintings in heavy gilded frames, and huge rococo mirrors, while through the tall, arched windows passers-by might glimpse the shimmer of some of the immense crystal chandeliers suspended from the high ceilings of one of the most splendid imperial residences ever to have existed.

Princess Marina's devoted nanny wrote to friends at home in England:

> Everything is exquisite. My nurseries consist of eight beautifully furnished rooms; dining-room, two saloon anterooms, night-nursery, dressing-room, bathroom and so on. There must be a regular army of servants here; it is a huge place. The King's palace in Athens is supposed to be big, but it is nothing like this. We are such a distance from the Grand Duchess's rooms that when I take the children along to their mother I have to wait for them. It is too far to go again to fetch them.

Astounded though she might have been by the scale and luxury of the Grand Duchess Vladimir's life, Miss Fox was not entirely enamoured of the Grand Duchess herself – 'that majestic personality', as Consuelo Vanderbilt, Duchess of Marlborough, once described her. Foxy's ideas of hygiene, as mentioned earlier, did not meet with the Grand Duchess's approval, and it was to her extreme vexation that, during the Nicholases' first winter visit, she discovered that her granddaughters' nurse insisted on flinging open the carefully fastened windows of the nursery suite. Not one to have the bitter night air wreak havoc with the almost tropical temperature inside the palace, the Grand Duchess went in person to fasten the windows and put Foxy firmly in her place. No less obstinate than Marie Pavlovna herself, however, Miss Fox immediately reopened all the windows the very moment the Grand Duchess's back was turned. From then on the defiant nurse was ever referred to as 'that dreadful woman'.

Imperious though the Grand Duchess Vladimir could be, she

was always a doting grandmother, showering gifts of all kinds on Olga, Elizabeth and Marina. Toys and dresses, items of jewellery, even ponies, were lovingly bestowed on the young princesses. Another treat, always guaranteed to delight, was when the Grand Duchess took Marina and her sisters into her dressing room to show them her spectacular collection of jewels. Displayed in special glass cases were a host of diadems and tiaras – including one composed of diamond hoops set with drop pearls, now in the possession of Queen Elizabeth ii – numerous parures, necklaces, chokers, earrings, bracelets and brooches, all containing flawless gems that covered the whole spectrum of precious and semi-precious stones.

If visits to St Petersburg were tempered, no matter how unintentionally, by an element of formality, the ambience of the Grand Duchess's home in the 'Imperial Village' at Tsarskoe Selo erred very much on the side of leisure and informality. It was here, too, that Marina and her sisters saw much of their uncles, the Grand Duke Kyrill, eldest of Princess Nicholas's three brothers (his wife Princess Victoria-Melita, once married to Ernst, Grand Duke of Hesse, brother of the Empress Alexandra, was another of Marina's godparents); the Grand Duke Boris; and the Grand Duke Andrei, who later married the Russian prima ballerina Mathilde Kschessinska, former mistress of the prince who became Tsar Nicholas ii. More or less the princesses' own age and, therefore, frequent holiday companions were the Tsarevitch Alexis and his four sisters, Olga, Tatiana, Marie and Anastasia, children of the Tsar and Tsarina. It was while playing with the younger Grand Duchesses at the Alexander Palace that Marina is believed to have seen the black-robed figure of the *staretz* Gregory Rasputin, whom she is said to have watched gravely as he raised his hand in blessing over the imperial children.

Such were Princess Marina's earliest years, set against the backcloth of one of history's most opulent and powerful dynasties. On 28 August 1914, less than a month after Germany had declared war on Russia, the Princess, her parents and sisters bade farewell to their Romanov cousins for what was to be the last time. Come 1918 and the end of the First World War, few members of the imperial family would still be alive.

Chapter Three

Shadows and Exile

The return journey to Greece at the end of that last Russian holiday in 1914 contrasted sharply with the arrival of Prince and Princess Nicholas and their children only a few weeks earlier. Travelling back through Russia, this time aboard a crowded, stuffy train, the family's progress was made even longer and more uncomfortable by repeated delays as their train was halted or shunted into sidings, to permit heavily laden troop trains free and urgent passage.

In Romania, where Prince and Princess Nicholas and their daughters rested briefly at the palace of Pelichor, King Carol put a special train at their disposal. But by the time they had crossed from Romania to Serbia, Marina and her sisters, weary and hot, had started to become fractious. 'The heat was unbearable,' Prince Nicholas recalled. 'We had no water and the children cried, until at a railway station we were able to purchase a watermelon with which to quench their thirst.' Many years later, Princess Marina clearly remembered the discomforts of that journey, 'the heat and the flies and the long dreary day, and eventually the watermelon that tasted so good'.

Not so good, once the family reached the frontier between Serbia and Bulgaria, was the discovery that both their luggage and their servants had disappeared. Exasperated though Prince and Princess Nicholas must have been, the young princesses helped to soothe frayed nerves by cavorting about in diaphanous nightdresses, loaned to them by the wife of the local stationmaster. In her biography of Princess Marina published in 1937, Baroness Helena von der Hoven wrote: 'Those garments were not exactly of the Paris model type, and raised peals of laughter when one of the three sisters simply disappeared in its voluminous folds or tripped over its trailing hem.'

One final stop at Salonika broke the family's tedious journey home to Athens. This time, though, the interruption was one of choice rather than of necessity. It took the form of a private pilgrimage, one which evoked memories of triumph as well as tragedy. In 1912 Greece had engaged Turkey, its old and most bitter enemy, in a battle over sovereignty. The campaign itself was brief, lasting no more than a few weeks. At the end of it the Greek Army, under the command of Prince Nicholas's brother Constantine, secured a decisive victory which culminated in the seizure of the vital Macedonian seaport of Salonika, over which Prince Nicholas himself was later appointed Military Governor. Freed from the tyrannical rule of their Turkish oppressors, the people celebrated in a frenzy of near-hysteria, welcoming the Greek Crown Prince as a hero and throwing themselves to the ground in front of his horse. No less jubilant was Constantine's father King George I. Greatly loved though he was by his people, the King had already announced his intention to abdicate the following year in favour of his eldest son. His family tried to dissuade him, but he was firmly resolved to hand the Greek crown to a younger man. 'I shall have reigned for fifty years', he said, 'and it's long enough for any king. I think I'm entitled to a little rest in my old age. Besides, Tino will be able to do far more with the country than I ever could. He has been born and bred here, while I am always a foreigner.'

Foreigner or not, the Greek victory at Salonika represented the greatest triumph of King George's entire reign. In honour of it, he decided to live there for a time, choosing a house on the shores of the Gulf of Thermai from which to rule. No king could ever have felt more secure in the affection of his people than George I, whose arrival in Salonika had been marked by overwhelming demonstrations of loyalty.

Four months later, on 18 March 1913, however, the still prevalent air of jubilation was shattered by the King's assassination. Accustomed to walking around Athens with exactly the same freedom enjoyed by the rest of his subjects, George I thought nothing of doing the same in Salonika, exchanging the time of day with all who greeted him. On the afternoon of his death, the King, accompanied only by an aide-de-camp, went out for his usual walk. Two hours or so later as they strode back, the King and his ADC passed a man leaning casually against a wall opposite a run-down café. Seconds later the man, described afterwards as a deranged Macedonian 'driven to desperation by sickness and want' drew a revolver from his pocket and shot the sixty-eight-year-old monarch in the back. His death was instantaneous.

Like the rest of her family, Princess Marina was heartbroken at the loss of her adored grandfather or 'Apapa', as she always called him. There is a story that when she learned of his death, Marina flung herself to the floor in an agony of grief. All attempts to console her were apparently to no avail, until Princess Nicholas told her youngest child, who had always been a particular favourite of the dead king, 'Apapa wouldn't want you to cry like that. Don't you remember that when you fell down he was always pleased if you were brave?'

George I was succeeded earlier than anyone could have anticipated by Crown Prince Constantine, Duke of Sparta, whose wife, the new Queen Sophie, was the sister of Germany's megalomaniac Kaiser Wilhelm II. Of the eldest of his brothers Prince Christopher wrote:

> No Sovereign was ever more popular than Constantine in the early days of his reign. The Greeks, romantic and impressionable, were ready to idolise the soldier King who had fought side by side with his men, shared camp life with them and led them to victory. He had liberated South Macedonia, Epirus and the Aegean Islands from the Turkish yoke. They began to remember the old legend that Constantinople should be given back to Greece and the Christian Church restored there when a King Constantine and a Queen Sophie reigned in Athens. The tradition probably owed its origins to the fact that the last emperor to fall on the ramparts of Byzantium was named Constantine and his wife was Sophie, but the people had a touching faith in it.

The visions and hopes the Greeks invested in their new and popular king were boosted to new heights when, shortly after Constantine and his forces had vanquished the Turks, they routed the Bulgarians. Both Greece and Bulgaria had long claimed Salonika as their own and, in the aftermath of the Greek victory, relations between the two countries had been severely strained. Suddenly Bulgarian troops were mobilized; without any formal declaration of war they attacked Salonika. Once more Constantine emerged victorious. 'The welcome he received on his return to Athens was stupendous,' Prince Christopher wrote. 'Thanksgiving services were held in all the churches, crowds besieged the Palace, waiting for hours to get a glimpse of him. . . . The spring and summer of 1914 were the most carefree, the most prosperous Greece had ever known.'

It was in that same carefree state of mind that Prince and Princess Nicholas had set out for their usual summer holiday in Russia. But by the end of August that year, as they broke their homeward journey at Salonika to stand before the memorial that Queen Olga had erected to the memory of her murdered husband, King George I, concern at things to come overshadowed the thoughts of Prince Nicholas and his wife.

At the start of the Great War the Greek Government had voted for neutrality. It was a decision which the King, with his intimate knowledge of the by now depleted condition of his army, vigorously supported. However, one man, anxious to assume even greater power for himself, was determined that Greece should join forces with the Allies. This was King Constantine's prime minister. Eleftherios Venizelos. In his memoirs Prince Christopher of Greece painted a clear and menacing picture of the man whose malicious campaign against the King and Queen Sophie would result in the Greek royal family's first period of exile.

> Venizelos first came into prominence as the thorn in the side of my brother George who was appointed High Commissioner in Crete in 1898. The post was no sinecure, for Crete was a hotbed of intrigue even before Venizelos appeared out of the blue, a shabby young man with a fox-like smile and an amazing gift of oratory and a still greater gift of putting other people in his pocket. He could talk so convincingly that even my father, though diametrically opposed to many of his theories, had to admit that, after listening to him for an hour, he generally found himself being reluctantly convinced. He was never forceful or compelling; he was smooth as silk, gentle and obsequious, with a mind as agile as a rapier and a never-failing flow of

words. On brains less alert he had a hypnotic effect; he could sway crowds in whatever direction he wished and twist cabinets this way and that until they did not know their own minds. His campaign in Crete was so successful that my brother was driven out of the island.

Although fully aware of Venizelos's character, King Constantine, unlike most other members of the royal family, continued to trust him. It proved a fatal error of judgement, for in his eagerness to involve Greece in world war the Prime Minister and his supporters, including certain sections of the Greek press, were determined to remove the King from his throne. To this end Venizelos needed no better excuse than the Queen's nationality. That she and her brother, the Kaiser, disliked each other with an intensity that almost bordered on hatred, that Sophie had been forbidden ever to set foot on German soil after she had embraced the Greek Orthodox faith, mattered not at all. It still meant that Venizelos could accuse King Constantine of pro-German sympathies and embellish this slander with rumours that Queen Sophie was in communication with German submarines via a secret wireless installation at Tatoi. So persistent, so damning was Venizelos's campaign that the King's popularity – and, as a consequence, that of all the royal family – plummeted.

At the age of ten Princess Marina knew nothing of politics, nor of the intrigue enveloping her family. When she saw rival factions openly brawling in the streets, she naturally asked what they were fighting for.

'Some are fighting for the King,' she was told, 'some against him.'

'But they all loved him so,' Marina argued; 'why have they changed like that?'

Bewildering as the answer was, it illustrated only too well how easily a volatile people like the Greeks could be manipulated by unscrupulous politicians such as Venizelos. While Marina was completely bemused by what little she saw and heard, she was devastated by one particular incident which was the direct result of Venizelist propaganda. Outraged by allegations of Queen Sophie's covert activities, arsonists made an assault on Tatoi. Sixteen people and untold numbers of animals perished in the blaze, which engulfed the forest and razed the palace itself to the ground.

The summer of 1916 had been especially dry and, on that day, a humidity of only 3 per cent had been recorded. Even the birds perched in the trees of the parched forest were silent.

Marina, her mother and sisters watched the red glow on the horizon from the house Prince Nicholas had taken for part of that summer at Kephisia in the foothills of Mount Pentelikon, midway between Athens and Tatoi. Meanwhile, King Constantine and a party of estate workers fought the fire until it threatened to surround them. Then, calling to his men to follow, he made off in the direction of a goat track he hoped would still be passable. The King and some of his party, including his youngest son Paul, later King Paul i, managed to find their way through the dense, choking smoke. Those who died had been trapped by flames or asphyxiated. Queen Sophie's own escape was no less dramatic. Scooping up her three-year-old daughter Katherine, she ran for a mile and a half until, exhausted and terrified, she was picked up by a passing car and driven to the safety of Prince Nicholas's villa at Kephisia.

That night Marina sobbed for the fawns and wild creatures of the forest, and for her 'pet' animals at the home farm. She wept, too, at the thought that her grandfather's tomb might have been destroyed. 'Have they burnt my darling Apapa?' she asked. The answer proved to be no, but of the 40,000-acre estate no more than a quarter survived the blaze.

Despite the destruction of Tatoi and the awful loss of life, Prime Minister Venizelos remained unrepentant and unmoved. As the situation deteriorated, Allied warships blockaded the port at Piraeus. In October 1916 Britain and France, furious that King Constantine continued to resist their entreaties to bring Greece into the war, issued an ultimatum. Two months later on 2 December, Allied troops, believing that the King had finally capitulated, marched into Athens. The strength of the resistance they met forced them to retreat, but that afternoon French battleships opened fire and for three hours bombarded Athens without respite. Shells exploded near the royal palace, sending the King and Queen together with their household down into the cellars, while in a street nearby Prince Christopher, frantically trying to get his car started, found that he had become the target of snipers. 'Mercifully there were some poor shots in Athens then!' he casually remarked afterwards.

At the Nicholas Palace the Princesses Marina, Olga, and Elizabeth rushed to the windows of the top-floor nursery from where, with mingled terror and excitement, they watched the street violence below. It was not until a horrified Princess Nicholas discovered them transfixed by the bloody scenes of fighting that Marina and her sisters were ushered swiftly to the basement to sit out the attack.

Six months later, in June 1917, King Constantine's abdication was formally requested. This he flatly refused, choosing instead to go into exile with his eldest son and rightful heir, Prince George. Thus the crown of the Hellenes passed to the King's second son, Alexander, who was ostensibly to reign in a temporary capacity until the return of his father. In the event, however, Alexander I was no more than a hostage of the Venizelist junta, a puppet king. 'His crown was a mockery,' Prince Christopher later remarked, 'but he wore it with dignity.' Entirely alone, the twenty-three-year-old King, who was to occupy the Greek throne until his untimely death little more than three years later, was kept under constant surveillance. His household was chosen for him and any 'courtiers' who were seen to become too friendly were summarily dismissed. Yet perhaps the cruellest deprivation of all for the young monarch was the total loss of communication with his exiled family. Even when he lay dying, his distracted mother Queen Sophie was consistently refused permission to return to Greece and her son's bedside.

In 1917 King Constantine's departure from Greece was all but prevented by the wailing crowds of loyal subjects who, like 'bewildered children', were massed on the landing stage and on the beach of the village of Oropos on the Gulf of Euboea. Prince Nicholas wrote:

> The nearer the King and Queen drew to the boat, the fiercer grew the frenzy of the people who tried to keep him back by force. Many leaped into the sea and held fast to the boat .... Among lamentations and sobs that rent the air the boat set slowly off, whilst all the people went down on their knees and stretched out their hands towards the King and Queen. It was a heartrending picture.

Of the uneasy, almost sepulchral mood in Athens itself Prince Christopher later wrote:

> . . . the once gay little capital was like the city of the dead.
> No one went out in the streets, all the theatres and shops
> were closed. Those of us of the royal family who remained
> behind lived in an atmosphere of suspicion. Everyone
> known to have been faithful to King Constantine was put
> under arrest. Men and women in all walks of life –
> statesmen, lawyers, writers, officers of both Army and Navy
> – were mysteriously denounced, hauled before a tribunal
> and sentenced, some to years of imprisonment, others to
> banishment in remote islands.

Banishment was also the fate of the entire royal family save, of
course, the new King Alexander. On 4 July 1917 Princess Marina
and her family, accompanied by Prince Christopher, and followed
by Prince and Princess Andrew and their four daughters, sailed
away from Athens at the start of their first journey into exile.
Initially short of ready cash and reliant on the generosity of loyal
friends, the royal party made their way to Switzerland. For the
next three years they divided their time between Zurich and
Lucerne, where they spent their summers, and St Moritz, where
they lived in winter.

Given the privileged existences to which they, like royalty the
world over, had always been accustomed, Prince and Princess
Nicholas felt the sting of exile rather more keenly than did their
children. With the adaptability of youth Marina, then aged eleven,
and Olga and Elizabeth, aged fourteen and thirteen respectively,
regarded Switzerland as a new adventure and, notwithstanding
occasional pangs of homesickness, soon became acclimatized to
their surroundings. For Marina with her nascent talent as a water-
colourist Switzerland proved inspirational. Under the tutelage of
a professional art teacher, she was soon interpreting the crisp
beauty of the countryside through her paintbox. No less diverting
was the awakening of new interests. Among them, in due season,
were winter sports including skiing, skating and tobogganing.

For Marina's parents, uncles and aunts, however, Switzerland
was not so great an adventure. Despite the relative tranquillity
of the country amid the mayhem of war and political upheaval
in the rest of Europe, the Greek royal family were still regarded
with the deepest suspicion. 'Here in the calm and peacefulness
of this neutral country', Prince Nicholas later recalled, 'we were

still marked down as dangerous, political intriguers who had to be closely watched, and shunned by everyone belonging to the Entente nations.' As if such thinly-veiled hostility were not enough, the royal family were also to suffer humiliation in other ways. They were not allowed to leave the country; friends could only visit them in strict secrecy; while their mail, though harmless enough in itself, was invariably censored. Even the children's adored nurse, Miss Fox, fell victim to Venizelist propaganda. She was summoned before the British Consul and warned that, unless she resigned her position with the 'traitors', and returned immediately to England, her passport would be confiscated. Like her three charges and their parents, Foxy was outraged. One day, she told the princesses as she prepared to leave, she would come back to them. When peace finally returned, Foxy fulfilled that promise.

Uncomfortable though their years in exile were, Prince and Princess Nicholas faced their ordeal with admirable stoicism. Even so, most of the claims made by romantic sympathizers in later years – that the Nicholas family experienced nothing but hardship and penury – are extremely difficult to accept as fact. Until their return to Greece, Prince and Princess Nicholas were certainly obliged to live strictly within their means, carefully monitoring their expenditure and rarely able to afford anything that might be considered a luxury. But at no time could they have been considered poor. Before long Prince Nicholas determined to help supplement his family's resources, and he did it in a highly practical way. Declaring that he painted 'at least as well as Mr Winston Churchill', he rented a studio in the Montreux suburb of Territet and, using the pseudonym 'Nicholas le Prince', succeeded in staging his first exhibition. His paintings not only sold well on that occasion but went on selling thereafter; a testimony to the Prince's abilities which confirmed his unshakeable belief in traditional art forms. He said at the time,

> Modern art goes on and on with all other modern atrocities grafted on our system by the lovers of neurotic disorder . . . for, instead of seeking to express in form, colour, and sound all that is beautiful, which lifts the spirit and mind to a sphere of higher perfection, it lends itself to a degrading manifestation of coarseness and vulgarity.

Prince Nicholas's pleasure at having become a commercially successful painter was naturally shared by every member of his family, but particularly by his youngest daughter, Marina. In years to come she, too, would find her own work – including portraits of her sisters, her daughter Alexandra, and her husband's niece Princess Margaret – hung in public exhibitions or reproduced in such popular journals as *Vogue*.

Another of the Prince's greatest pleasures throughout his life was the company of his family. At home in Greece, Sundays had always been set aside for informal family gatherings at the royal palace. Even in exile the royal family continued to see a great deal of one another, though concern for the precarious health of King Constantine and constant anxiety for the well-being of the captive King Alexander in Athens meant that family get-togethers in Switzerland were sometimes rather melancholy affairs.

For Prince Nicholas and his brothers, as well as for Princess Nicholas, there was further anxiety over the welfare of their respective mothers, the dowager Queen Olga of the Hellenes and the Grand Duchess Vladimir of Russia. Shortly before the outbreak of revolution in 1917, both women – one a Russian Grand Duchess by birth, the other a Grand Duchess by marriage – had become involved with newly established military hospitals. That which Queen Olga had been invited to open was a converted palace at Pavlovsk, not far from Tsarskoe Selo, while the hospital run by the Grand Duchess Vladimir was situated at Kislovodsk, a famous spa in the Caucasus. With the start of the Russian Revolution Queen Olga and the Grand Duchess Vladimir were suddenly marooned. To begin with, Queen Olga's family, as Prince Christopher put it, tended to imagine 'that she would be perfectly safe among the people who had known her since childhood'. In the event, however, the dowager Queen, all but alone in a country where royalty was being rounded up like so many sheep ready for the slaughter, was far from safe. Through the long and strenuous efforts of the Danish embassy in St Petersburg, or Petrograd as it had been renamed at the beginning of the war, Queen Olga was able to leave Russia and, in July 1918, was finally reunited with her family. Prince Christopher recalled in his memoirs:

My mother was only the ghost of her old self when she

joined us in Switzerland. The months of worry and suspense and the privations she had undergone had worn her to skin and bone. The events in Greece had tortured her with anxiety, far away from us all as she was and unable even to get accurate news; and in addition she had had the grief of losing seventeen members of her family . . . in the Russian Revolution. . . . Like everyone else who came out of Russia she was half starved, for a diet of bread soaked in oil . . . is not exactly nourishing and it was some time before she recovered her health.

Harrowing though Queen Olga's experiences had been, she fared rather better than the Grand Duchess Vladimir, whose own escape was not effected until the early summer of 1920. For three years the Grand Duchess, whose house at Kislovodsk was said to have been searched no fewer than twenty-two times, managed to keep one step ahead of the Bolsheviks who sought her. More than once she fled into the mountains; then General Wrangel, the White Russian commander, explained that he could no longer guarantee her safety. Without further delay the Grand Duchess was put aboard a train bound for the Black Sea port of Novorossisk. During the entire journey, which lasted seven weeks, this grandest of all Grand Duchesses found herself occupying a tiny compartment cheek by jowl with a number of other desperate refugees. Their only form of sustenance was soup thickened with black bread; they slept how and wherever they could, while sanitation was so primitive as to be almost non-existent.

At Novorossisk, after a further agonizing delay, the Grand Duchess Vladimir boarded an Italian ship bound for Venice. From there, travelling via Paris, the Grand Duchess finally arrived in Switzerland. Like Queen Olga, the indomitable Marie Pavlovna stepped down from her train at Montreux a physical wreck. At the age of sixty-six the Grand Duchess, now white-haired and thinner than her family could ever recall seeing her, was utterly worn out by her long ordeal. To Princess Marina and her sisters, the grandmother they now saw again for the first time in six years was but a pathetic shadow of the beautiful, exquisitely-dressed woman whose company they revelled in and whom they had last seen in St Petersburg at the very start of the Great War. Though dispossessed of everything she had once owned, the Grand

Duchess Vladimir soon proved to her daughter and three grand-children that her robust sense of humour had been salvaged intact. For several weeks the Grand Duchess enjoyed the hospitality of her family. Then, in the hope of restoring her health, she left them for her favourite spa at Contrexéville in France. It was there, only two months later, on 6 September 1920, that she died.

Sudden though the demise of Grand Duchess was – perhaps even ironic, given that she had narrowly escaped death at the hands of the Bolsheviks – Marie Pavlovna had enjoyed a full and undeniably spectacular life. That her end should have been has-tened by events of the recent past may have seemed tragic to those closest to her, yet in Greece at that time a far more tragic incident was about to claim a life which, in many ways, had hardly begun.

Chapter Four

A Brief Return

One month after the death of the Grand Duchess Vladimir news reached the exiled royal family that the young King Alexander lay dying. Shocked and incredulous, they heard how the King had spent some of his time on that fateful day tinkering with his motorbike on the Tatoi estate and how, still wearing a greasy mechanic's overall, he had then taken his Alsatian dog for a walk, pausing on his way back to call in at the cottage of the keeper of the vineyards and his wife. It was there that Alexander's dog was attacked by one of the keeper's pet monkeys. As the King tried to pull it away, the monkey turned on him and bit him on the arm and ankle. Horrified, the keeper's wife did all she could to clean and dress the wounds, before summoning a doctor from Athens. Despite medical attention, however, the King's fate was already sealed and that same night blood poisoning set in.

Frantic with alarm, Queen Sophie begged repeatedly to be allowed to return to Greece to comfort her son. All her pleas were rejected. Finally, in utter despair, she asked if her mother-in-law, the dowager Queen Olga, might be allowed to go in her place. Miraculously, or so it seemed to her family, this request was granted, and the elderly queen set off immediately for Athens. On 25 October, twelve hours before his grandmother arrived, Alexander died, crying out in agonized delirium for his mother.

In a sense, the monkey's bite claimed two victims. The second, though only metaphorically, was the Prime Minister, Eleftherios Venizelos. For in permitting the return of Queen Olga he had failed to take into account the wealth of popular feeling that for half a century had warmly surrounded the widow of Greece's

31

much loved King George I. A general election had already been called in Greece for 15 November 1920, less than two weeks after Prince Paul had been offered – and had refused – the crown of his dying brother. When the votes were counted Venizelos, convinced that he would be returned, was shattered to discover that he had suffered the most crushing defeat. Of the 370 seats in the Greek Parliament, the Venizelists had won only 120.

Amid general rejoicing the new Prime Minister, Dimitrios Ralli, who had always been an ardent royalist, asked to see the Queen Dowager. So overcome was he when he knelt to kiss her hand that Queen Olga urged him to rise. When he refused, she too went down on her knees, assuring him that she would not get up unless he did. The purpose of Ralli's emotional mission was to offer the Queen the regency of Greece, pending the return of the rightful sovereign King Constantine.

The sense of euphoria in Greece at this turn of events not surprisingly transmitted itself to the royal family in Switzerland. The King, however, wisely tempered joy with caution and decided that a plebiscite should be held in order to gauge the feeling among his subjects. Early in December 1,010,788 votes were cast, out of which only 10,883 were found to oppose the monarchy's complete restoration.

Shortly before Christmas that year a welcome which can only be described as ecstatic greeted the return of King Constantine and Queen Sophie to Greece. Among those of the royal family who had taken the first opportunity to return home were Prince and Princess Nicholas and their three daughters. Flowers, telegrams and messages of congratulation without number awaited the family at the Nicholas Palace. A few days later, on 19 December, Queen Olga headed the royal reception committee in Athens which received the King and Queen themselves. Prince Nicholas wrote:

> The royal train had been shunted on to a side-line which, running through one of the streets, ended at a small square, where we awaited its arrival. When they saw it coming about a mile off, the people could not contain their emotion. The cry *'Erchetai! Erchetai!'* (He is coming! He is coming!) – which had been the password ever since they heard that the King was on his way to Greece – rose like the roar of an ocean

wave. The engine, all beflagged, was painfully ploughing its way through a seething mass of people yelling, crying, gesticulating, sobbing hysterically. Men were hanging on to the engine and the steps of the carriage like flies. Slowly the train crawled to its destination, and came to a halt in front of where our mother stood. She stepped first into the carriage, and we followed her to greet the King. It would be impossible to describe his emotion; imagine what deep sorrows he had been through, and what this spontaneous manifestation of loyalty and love from his people meant to him!

When the King and Queen alighted and had to walk a distance of about twenty yards to reach their carriage, they were literally assaulted, almost crushed, by a population driven mad by uncontrollable joy. To keep order, or protect the King against any danger, was out of the question, but then, could he be better guarded than by the people who loved him!

As the royal carriage slowly advanced it was all the coachman and grooms could do to control the six horses in this maddened crowd. But step by step they moved onwards, the carriage almost lifted off the ground by the people pressing against it from all sides; and so great was their desire to assure themselves that this was not a dream, but that their sovereign was actually again in their midst, that they hung on to the sides of the carriage and stretched out their hands to him, whilst tears streamed down their faces.

Though they could not have guessed it, then, the royal family's happiness at their return to Greece was to be short lived. On the horizon yet more storm clouds – a legacy of the Venizelist years – were already gathering, while beyond stretched the prospect of another, and longer, exile for the Greek royal family. At the end of 1920, however, thoughts of trouble were far from royal minds. What concerned them all was to re-establish the pattern of their lives in the comfortable mould of earlier times.

For Princess Marina, another birthday – which she always observed on 13 December according to the Julian calendar – led her to the threshold of womanhood. At fourteen she was a tall, slender girl with rich, brown hair, framing a clear-skinned, oval face. Indeed, her striking good looks, for which she was later to become world-renowned, had already started to turn heads. Friends of her parents constantly remarked upon such features as her high cheekbones or wide, amber-coloured eyes, while her smile, though somewhat crooked, was invariably described throughout her life as 'enchanting'. In later years her voice – to some fascinating, to others guttural and unbecoming – was both deep and husky. Her speech was clipped and staccato, and her accent, sometimes described as 'slightly Greek', was, in fact, as unmistakably Russian as her mother's.

To the delight of Marina and her family, the welcome return of Miss Fox in the capacity of loyal and valued retainer added strength to the growing sense of normality both in Athens and at the recently rebuilt palace at Tatoi. For Marina in particular, however, normality also meant a tedious return to schoolroom routine. Yet, as with all young people, pleasurable diversions outweighed more onerous occupations and in Marina's far from drab life two events in 1921 gave rise to great excitement. On 10 March, Princess Helen – or 'Sitta', as she was known – the eldest of King Constantine's three daughters, was married to Crown Prince Carol of Romania (afterwards King Carol II); then in Corfu, exactly three months later, on 10 June, Marina's thirty-six-year-old aunt Princess Andrew, the former Princess Alice of Battenberg, gave birth to her fifth child and only son, Philip, now the Duke of Edinburgh.

It was also at about this time that Princess Marina's lifelong friendship with Princess Juliana of the Netherlands (Queen Juliana from 1948 until her abdication in 1980) first began. Juliana, who was three years younger than Marina, had recently developed an interest in philately. In order to acquire Greek stamps for her collection, her mother, Queen Wilhelmina, suggested that Juliana should write to the youngest of Prince Nicholas's daughters. In time the rapport which the two princesses established as penfriends ripened to such an extent that, as they grew up, they often visited one another; and when, in 1934, Marina married, she invited the Dutch princess to act as one of her bridesmaids. Later still, during the 1960s, Marina's name appeared high on the guest list at celebrations marking Juliana's silver wedding anniversary, and, in

August 1968, though the occasion could hardly have contrasted more sharply, the Queen of the Netherlands was among a large contingent of foreign royal figures who travelled to Windsor to attend Princess Marina's funeral service at St George's Chapel.

But, to return to the years of Marina's youth, it is clear that her growing sophistication did nothing to stifle her sense of humour or, indeed, her enthusiasm for enjoying life. One example of the Princess's sense of fun was revealed by Baroness Helena von der Hoven, who wrote of a particular game Marina and some of her cousins always enjoyed. Played out on a smaller island adjoining Spetsai, the game was called 'Keeping House'. The 'house' itself was a favourite fig tree. The Baroness wrote:

> One crossed in a sailing boat to this island and picnicked on the beach. Then one climbed the tree. Each member of the party had her own branch which represented her 'room' and all the figs on this branch were entirely her property. One could visit each other and exchange fruit which was carefully passed over on fresh green leaves. It needed a lot of agility not to drop any and if such a misfortune happened it was greeted with a lot of merry laughter and jokes.
>
> Though one of the youngest, Princess Marina was always the ringleader and kept the company in fits of laughter by mimicking her governess of whom she gave striking imitations. There were also other pranks which necessitated a certain amount of tactics and daring, and her contemporaries learnt to know so well that humorous, half-wistful, half-mischievous smile of the young Princess Marina.
>
> One of the favourite games in those days was shooting arrows. The bows were home-made out of flexible branches tied firmly with a bit of string and great competition took place as to who should produce the best weapon. It was great fun hiding behind trees and rocks and shooting at invisible enemies, and Robin Hood and other similar heroes were very popular at that time.

Away from the realm of make-believe there were few heroes in the Greece of the early 1920s for Princess Marina and her cousins to emulate. In January 1921, though much against the King's wishes, Greek forces had again been mobilized to take on the

Turks, this time over the question of sovereignty in Asia Minor. That war, which lasted until September 1922, resulted in the wholesale slaughter of much of the Greek Army. Over 300,000 troops, including King Constantine and his brothers Nicholas and Andrew, had gone into battle, marching, as Prince Christopher put it, 'staight into the wasps' nest prepared by that military genius, Mustafa Kemal'. Inevitably someone had to shoulder the blame for the decimation of Greek forces at Smyrna, and that someone, conveniently, perhaps obviously, was King Constantine himself.

In the meantime with her husband away at war, and Marina on what was to be a prolonged visit to England in the company of Miss Fox, Princess Nicholas accepted an invitation to stay with her brother-in-law Prince Christopher and his American wife Nancy at their house in Cannes. With her went the princesses Olga and Elizabeth.

It was while in Cannes during that spring of 1922 that Princess Olga met and became engaged to her kinsman Crown Prince Frederick of Denmark, the twenty-three-year-old son of King Christian x. At that time, Olga, with her slim form and delicate features, was arguably the most attractive of Prince Nicholas's daughters. Before too long she would even find herself described in the press as the 'most beautiful princess in Europe', though since the very same would one day be said of her sister Marina, it was, perhaps, a rather fatuous compliment to have been paid. Nevertheless, Crown Prince Frederick, or 'Rico', as he was known, was greatly enamoured and attentively 'paid court', as it was known in those days, to the young Princess. For her part, Olga was completely overwhelmed by the speed with which she had been wooed and apparently won, for, as Neil Balfour – who became her son-in-law in 1969 – explained, 'She was just nineteen and though in behaviour and manner well trained and therefore seemingly grown up and sophisticated, she was at heart a child, romantic and vulnerable ... a pious teenager, conscious of her role as the eldest daughter and longing to think "the right thoughts" and feel "the right feelings".'

As the weeks slipped by, however, and hopes for a late summer wedding began to fade, it started to become painfully clear that Prince Frederick's ardour was already beginning to cool. Then suddenly, as Olga's uncle Prince Christopher put it, a 'misunderstanding arose'. That misunderstanding, as friends of Princess Marina later interpreted it, had much to do with Prince Frederick's addiction to alcohol. It has even been said that when Rico and Olga appeared in public on one occasion, the Prince was so completely drunk that, instead of taking his fiancée's hand in his own to acknowledge the cheers of a small crowd, he raised that of Olga's sister Elizabeth instead. It is difficult to know whether that incident alone constituted the sudden 'misunderstanding' Prince Christopher referred to, but quite obviously something fairly serious had occurred to cause a rift between the couple. That September Rico and Olga agreed to meet in order to discuss the future. On 8 September the bewildered Princess, who might have become Queen of Denmark, confided to her diary 'If only I knew what a state of mind he is in! Is he still bitter and resolved to break off the engagement? I only hope he will listen to me and after that if he still remains the same it means he never really loved me!' Three days later Rico and Olga talked together for three-quarters of an hour, but, wrote the Princess, '. . . he had quite made up his mind to give it up. I said I was willing to try again but he said he had no more love for me (it couldn't have been very strong while it was there).'

Upsetting though the whole sorry episode had undoubtedly been for both the Greek and Danish royal families, it cannot be said the Princess Olga had lost her ideal husband. Neil Balfour wrote:

> The pressure was certainly there for the engagement to continue, and though Olga had tried to steel herself for the occasion, she was inevitably apprehensive. She had scarcely had time to fall in love with Rico, but she had enjoyed the flattery and attention and had responded in all the established ways. She had subsequently realized that her dreams of a romantic love affair . . . ending happily ever after in marriage were an illusion.

At a family gathering soon after Princess Olga's engagement had officially ended, the inevitable post-mortem was interrupted by the sixteen-year-old Princess Marina. Sitting quietly sketching by a window, she had all but been forgotten by the adults locked in earnest discussion until a voice demanded, 'Why the hell should Olga marry him if she doesn't love him! I wouldn't.' Princess

Nicholas turned to Prince Christopher and smiled: 'Out of the mouths of babes. . . .' One year later Olga did marry for love; but a further thirteen years were to pass before the Crown Prince of Denmark, later King Frederick ix, took a wife. In May 1935 he finally married Princess Ingrid, only daughter of King Gustav vi Adolf of Sweden.

Marina's visit to England during the spring and early summer of 1922 caused her to miss the initial excitement of her sister's ill-starred engagement. Yet, when she and Foxy arrived in London, staying first at a hotel in Kensington and later at a country house in Warlingham, Surrey, there was more than enough family news to catch up with. Visiting Queen Mary at Windsor and Queen Alexandra at Sandringham, for example, meant hearing all about Princess Mary's wedding that February to Henry, Viscount Lascelles, and through letters, postcards and Foreign Office dispatches following the progress of Edward, Prince of Wales – 'David' to his family – who was then on an official tour of the Far East.

For Marina, as for the rest of her family, it was a pleasurable relief to travel without restrictions after their enclosed years in Switzerland. But to travel through choice was one thing, to wander as an exile quite another. The disastrous campaign in Asia Minor concluded that September meant that, when Marina rejoined her family, she did so as a refugee once more. In 1922 Greece had demanded – and this time secured – the abdication of King Constantine. Then, as before, those in power expelled the royal family save all but two of its members: Prince George, who now became King George ii, and the ex-King's brother Prince Andrew.

Seeking vengeance against those considered to have instigated the war, disillusioned army officers arrested several prominent ministers. Shortly afterwards Prince Andrew, now back at home at his villa Mon Repos on the island of Corfu, was requested to travel to Athens in order to give evidence at the ministers' trial. No sooner had he arrived than he himself was arrested and marched off to prison, accused of having helped instigate the war with Turkey.

Among his family – now in Italy at the start of their second exile – concern for the Prince was exacerbated by the fact that all communication with him was forbidden. His guards, as his brother Christopher recalled, 'kept the strictest watch and confiscated all letters and parcels. . . . Even food sent in by sympathizers was closely examined and a *foie gras* in aspic, with which a dear old lady intended to console him, was hacked to pieces before he was allowed to eat it.' Finally, in a desperate attempt to make contact with the prisoner, Prince Christopher

> . . . hit on the happy expedient of writing a letter on cigarette-paper, rolling it tightly and putting it with other cigarettes into his valet's case. In this way it reached him safely. He answered it with a short note full of courage, but reading between the lines I knew that he had no longer any hope of regaining his freedom. He had just had a conversation with his former school friend, M. Pangalos, now Minister of War and instigator of his trial, that had left him small grounds for optimism.
>
> 'How many children have you?' Pangalos had asked suddenly and, when my brother, surprised at the irrelevance of the question, told him he shook his head: 'Poor things, what a pity they will soon be orphans!'

Before long, each of the imprisoned ministers, powerless and without influence, was executed. Not so Prince Andrew, despite his doom-laden exchange with the new Minister of War. Entirely through the efforts of the royal family, representations were heard in high places. Princess Andrew dispatched appeals to several European heads of state; Queen Olga wrote to the kings of England and Spain; while Princess Christopher appealed to the Pope. All reacted sympathetically and urgently sent emissaries to Athens. Britain's King George v went one step further and, at his behest, the cruiser *Calypso* was ordered into the harbour at Phaleron. Days later Prince Andrew was freed; his inquisitors had decreed that he should be exiled, not shot.

Towards the end of what had been a deeply disturbing year Princess Nicholas, who had only recently recovered from diphtheria, left Paris – where she had stayed since the end of Olga's engagement – for Palermo. There she joined her husband, the ex-King and Queen, and other members of the royal family. When Princess Marina finally arrived with her sister Elizabeth after a short holiday in Chamonix, she immediately summed up everybody's feelings of dismay by saying – not without a touch of humour – 'We really needn't have unpacked our trunks.' For the next year or so Marina and her immediate family would find themselves packing and unpacking with increased regularity, until they eventually settled on somewhere permanent to live. Their travels had already begun in a small way after they grew restless in Palermo. At the end of October Princess Olga, lamenting her family's situation – 'one can hardly realize this is the second exile and we are once more like wandering Jews with no home to go to!' – had exchanged the Ritz in Paris for a 'Godforsaken ... perfectly foul' hilltop hotel in San Remo.

It was to that modest hostelry, which so displeased the ill-tempered Princess Olga, that Prince and Princess Nicholas travelled in December so that their family might be reunited in time for Christmas. Prevailing circumstances and relatively humble surroundings meant, of course, that Christmas 1922 was observed in a manner distinctly at odds with the kind of celebrations they had always been accustomed to. Yet if, as the New Year began, the Greek royal family were still bemoaning their fate instead of counting their blessings, one event did give rise to genuine sadness. In Palermo on 11 January 1923 King Constantine suffered a stroke and died. He was fifty-four.

The following month Prince and Princess Nicholas were on the move once again, this time to Merano in the Tyrol. With them went Marina and Elizabeth, on whom operations were to be performed for the removal of their adenoids. A few weeks later, while their younger daughters recuperated, Prince and Princess Nicholas took Olga to Florence, where, to her absolute delight, they spent three absorbing weeks visiting the palaces, museums and art galleries of which Prince Nicholas had so often spoken. By the beginning of April the whole family was together again at Merano and busily making plans to visit England. The idea that he should take his family to London for 'the season' had first been suggested to Prince Nicholas by his British cousin Princess Victoria, or 'Toria', as she was known. Hoping, perhaps, that Olga would attract the attentions of the Prince of Wales, the most eligible royal bachelor in all Christendom, Prince and Princess Nicholas, accompanied by their three excited daughters, left Merano on 31 May and eight days later booked in to the Granby Court Hotel in Queen's Gate, Kensington.

Chapter Five

Parisian Exile

For Prince and Princess Nicholas, as for their daughters Olga and Elizabeth, the summer season of 1923 was, in every way, a breathtaking merry-go-round of social engagements. There were lunches and dinners at Buckingham Palace, Claridge's, and the famous Embassy Club; balls hosted by Lady Zia Wernher, the Duchess of Sutherland, Sir Philip Sassoon, the Duchess of Portland, and the Red Cross; and sporting fixtures such as the tennis championships at Wimbledon, the Royal Horse Show, and polo matches at Roehampton, Ranelagh and Hurlingham. These were punctuated by tea and cocktail parties, visits to the theatre, a royal garden party and, as always when the Greek royal family were in England, expeditions to the most fashionable London shops and stores.

For Princess Olga there was also romance, though not with the British heir apparent. At the ball given by the Russian-born Lady Zia Wernher, Prince Paul of Yugoslavia saw and fell in love with Prince Nicholas's twenty-year-old daughter. Even though they had never met before and, indeed, were not even introduced that night, Prince Paul was so smitten that he contrived to get himself invited to all the functions Olga was most likely to attend. On 10 July, Paul achieved his objective, but appeared to make no great impression. At subsequent events he was infinitely more successful; so much so, in fact, that by 29 July, when they went to the cinema together, Olga correctly sensed the reason for Paul's apparent nervousness and, when he proposed, she unhesitatingly accepted.

Prince Paul of Serbia, as he was then known, had been born in St Petersburg on 15 April 1893, the only child of Prince Arsène

Karageorgevitch of Serbia and Aurore Demidoff, Princess of San Donato. A nephew of King Peter of Serbia, Paul, who would eventually become Regent of Yugoslavia – his state became part of Yugoslavia in 1929 – was educated in Switzerland and afterwards at Christ Church, Oxford, where he read Classics. As an undergraduate he lived in considerable style, employing two servants as well as a chauffeur to drive his Daimler limousine. Later, when he came down from Oxford, he took a flat in Mount Street, Mayfair, which he shared with Prince Serge Obolensky.

In spite of his background and unquestionable loyalty to Yugoslavia, Prince Paul was very much an anglophile. Not only was his outlook decidedly British, but so too were the majority of his closest friends, among whom were 'Bertie' and Elizabeth, Duke and Duchess of York, later King George VI and Queen Elizabeth.

During this visit to London Princess Marina's own activities may well have seemed uninspiring compared to those of her parents and sisters. Witnessing the Royal Tournament, for instance, even if it was from the comfort of the royal box, could not match the glamour of an event like the Duchess of Sutherland's fancy-dress ball. Yet for all that Marina, who was still too young to participate in high society's frolics, was content to watch from the sidelines.

Later that year, on Monday 22 October, Princess Olga married Prince Paul in the chapel of the Old Palace in Belgrade. Before the ceremony, conducted according to the rites of the Greek Orthodox church, 'Puppy' and 'Mummy', as Olga called her parents, blessed the bride with a holy picture. Then at midday the Minister of the Court arrived to lead Olga and her father in procession through the palace to the candle-lit chapel. At the altar Prince Paul, resplendent in ceremonial uniform, waited with his best man, the Duke of York. Among the congregation, in places of honour, sat Paul's cousin King Alexander of Serbia and his wife Marie, whose son Peter had been baptized only the day before; King Ferdinand and Queen Marie of Romania, the Serbian King's parents-in-law; the Duchess of York; and Princess Nicholas with Marina and Elizabeth. Also present was Queen Elisabeth of Greece, wife of the bride's uncle King George II and eldest daughter of the Romanian king and his outrageously flamboyant consort Queen Marie.

This gathering marked the end of a relatively settled period in the fortunes of the family. Two months later, in December 1923, Greece was to be declared a republic, and the King and Queen sent into exile. George II and Queen Elisabeth, like the rest of the royal family, were to be homeless once more. It was not until twelve years later, in November 1935, that the Greek monarchy would be restored yet again. But then Queen Elisabeth, disillusioned perhaps and understandably intolerant of Greece's ambivalent attitude towards its royal family, would not be among those who returned. In July that year, she and King George were to divorce. Queen Elisabeth would subsequently resume Romanian nationality in order to live on an estate of her own in Transylvania. There she would be content to stay until 1952, when she was to acquire a villa in Cannes, living there for another four years until her death at the age of sixty-two.

If Queen Elisabeth was to find happiness again in her native Romania – where she not only established a new hospital, but a children's home as well – the lot of her former husband was to be as turbulent as ever. In April 1941, the German invasion of Greece would force King George II to leave his country once more, only to be restored to the throne as the result of a plebiscite in September 1946. Seven months later, however, he was dead.

George II was to be succeeded on 1 April 1947 by Prince Paul, his sole surviving brother. The reign of King Paul I would certainly not be without incident, but as a wise and politically astute ruler, he knew how to maintain control of his kingdom and retain the respect of his people. After King Paul's untimely death on 6 March 1964, his only son – who became King Constantine II – was to occupy the Greek throne but briefly. The Colonels' coup of 1967 would force him, too, to flee the country and, following the restoration of democracy in 1973, a referendum would oppose his return. Today he lives in London with his wife Anne-Marie, youngest daughter of the very same King Frederick of Denmark who, as Crown Prince, had once been engaged to Princess Marina's sister Olga.

These events, however, lay in the unforeseeable future when, with the celebration of their eldest daughter's marriage at an end, and Paul and Olga themselves on honeymoon in Italy, enjoying the splendours of Venice, Florence and Rome, Prince and Princess Nicholas returned to Paris with Marina and Elizabeth.

Between leaving London at the close of the 1923 summer season

43

and setting out for Belgrade that October, the family had stayed briefly at the Campbell Hotel on the Avenue Friedland. But when Greece again became a republic, Prince and Princess Nicholas took the decision to make Paris their home. Almost immediately their search for suitable accommodation began. For a while they rented a furnished service flat near the Trocadero, but then discovered an unfurnished apartment of far better proportions in the Boulevard Jules Sandeau, near Porte de la Muette, which leads into the Bois de Boulogne.

Not long after the Greek royal family had begun their second exile, Prince Nicholas entered into negotiations with the proprietors of the Grand Bretagne, Athens's leading hotel. In shrewd anticipation of their interest, the Prince proposed offering a lease on his Athens mansion in return for a regular income that would help maintain his family during their absence. Within a matter of weeks a deal had been agreed and the Nicholas Palace, renamed Le Petit Palais, became a regal annex of the larger hotel. As a result of this arrangement some of the furnishings from their house in Athens were shipped to France, and with them Prince and Princess Nicholas set about creating a proper home for their daughters and themselves at their new apartment. As soon as they moved in, Marina and Elizabeth selected their own bedrooms and, to their delight, were given a separate sitting room. Here they could entertain friends and, of course, some of their cousins who, like them, were now Paris-based, without having to invade the rooms that Prince and Princess Nicholas had chosen for themselves.

Before long, in order to give form to his enforced leisure, the work of 'Nicholas Le Prince' began appearing once again in the Parisian art galleries. And once again Princess Marina's father was flattered by the number of commissions that flooded into his studio with, of course, the appropriate fees. Prince Nicholas was, as one observer put it, 'far more in his own element in the studios of the Left Bank and in the society of artists, writers and musicians, than in the round of official engagements which had filled his days in Athens'. We are also told that Princess Marina 'loved this Paris of the artist. Ever since her childhood in Athens, when she had run into her father's studio and coaxed him into letting her use his paints, they had shared an absorbing interest in art. Through all their adventures, even when her other lessons had been neglected, he had seen that she studied under the best teachers.'

Although Princess Marina was far more mature than many girls fast approaching the age of seventeen – and in those days young people were not nearly as streetwise as they are today – the disruptive influence of Greek politics meant that Marina's formal education was not nearly as complete as her mother would have wished. To remedy the situation, Princess Nicholas decided that a year at finishing school would be of benefit to her youngest daughter. The school the Princess chose at Auteuil had two immediate points in its favour. First it catered for the requirements of girls of all nationalities, and secondly it was run by a friend of the family, the Russian Princess Mestchersky. Not surprisingly, Marina herself was far from enthusiastic at the prospect of leaving home, and the very thought of regulated hours and strict discipline made her positively miserable. But since Princess Nicholas had presented her with a *fait accompli*, Marina's only alternative was to grit her teeth and get on with it.

'At first we didn't understand her,' said one of her school friends many years later. 'She had an air of reserve which we mistook for hauteur. Afterwards we realized that it was only shyness, and beneath it she was the most human person in the world.' Human though Princess Marina certainly was, this fundamental shyness, which even as an adult she never lost, would often be mistaken for hauteur. But since she was also perfectly capable of pulling rank and becoming immensely grand, particularly with those she considered inferior, it was an easy mistake to make. Among the girls at Princess Mestchersky's finishing school, however, Marina was invariably considered 'the tops'. It has been said that 'she would fly into battle in defence of some girl who was out of favour with the rest, not caring whether she made herself disliked or not. They were rather in awe of her sharp wit. Her knowledge of the world and of human nature made her seem different from themselves. . . .'

As a boarder, Princess Marina always began the day with prayers at 8 am, followed by breakfast half an hour later. At 9 she and the rest of the girls were allowed to walk in the Bois de Boulogne for an hour, until morning studies began. French language, history and literature, for example, might be followed by talks on subjects as diverse as China and Chinese art or the industrial development of Great Britain. Lunch was served promptly at 1 pm and until teatime, three and a half hours later, afternoons would be spent visiting places of interest such as the Louvre, Versailles or Fontainebleau. Lectures followed by 'prep' occupied the late afternoon, and dinner was always served on the stroke of 7.30 pm. After that, evenings would often be taken up with visits to the theatre or to concerts, not merely for the sake of entertainment, but to help broaden the girls' appreciation of the performing arts.

It was early in 1924, during her first term at Princess Mest-chersky's school, that Marina learned she was shortly to become an aunt. News that Olga was expecting her first child that August was rapturously received in Paris, and in May, when Prince and Princess Paul, as they were formally known, spent a fortnight at the Nicholas's apartment while *en route* to England, the family's obvious joy was sufficient cause for renewed celebrations.

Determined that he and Olga should spend the summer in England, where he was anxious for the baby to be born, Prince Paul rented Bisham Grange, a picturesque cottage near Marlow in Buckinghamshire, for the first six weeks of their visit. Then, at Ascot in June, during the traditional four-day race meeting that is a high point of the British royal family's year, the Duchess of York suggested that Paul and Olga might like to stay at White Lodge in Richmond Park during August and September for Olga's confinement. White Lodge – where Queen Mary had been born and where she, in turn, gave birth to her first child, the future King Edward VIII – had been given to the Duke and Duchess of York when they were married in April 1923. Prince Paul, over-whelmed by Elizabeth York's offer, immediately accepted.

On 7 August the expectant parents drove to Richmond and there, on the thirteenth, Olga gave birth to a son. One month later their absent hosts interrupted their annual summer holiday at Balmoral to attend the christening of the infant Prince Alexander. The ceremony at White Lodge, like Paul and Olga's wedding in Belgrade not quite a year before, was performed according to the rites of the Greek Orthodox Church. Princess Marina, together with her parents and sister Elizabeth, who were again in London for the 'season', were naturally among the guests at the christening; so, too, were King Alexander of Serbia and the Infanta Beatrice of Spain who, along with the Duke of York, stood as godparents to the four-week-old prince.

That summer Marina, now technically a débutante in her own right, took a more active part in the round of social events than had been permitted the previous year. The Curzons invited the family to stay with them at Hackwood near Ascot, the Portlands were their hosts at Welbeck, while Lord Ivor Churchill entertained them at Blenheim Palace. Then, as if in some children's story, the ball was suddenly over and it was time for the exiled Princess to return to Paris. Marina went back to school to finish her education, while Princess Nicholas continued her involvement with the relief agencies she had established to help ease the plight of Russian refugees, thousands of whom had settled in Paris after fleeing the Revolution. Of all the organizations which she had been instrumental in founding or was otherwise connected with in some way, Princess Nicholas was especially attached to two residential homes in particular. One of them had been set up by Lady Dorothy Paget, wealthy daughter of Lord Queensborough. Moved by the pitiful conditions in which ageing men and women, once members of the Russian imperial court, were now living, Dorothy Paget – who, like Princess Marina, also attended the Mestchersky school – bought a large country house at St Geneviève-des-Bois and opened it as a home for destitute courtiers. There, former ambassadors, ladies-in-waiting and suchlike sought refuge from reality and, in an atmosphere of tranquillity, relived faded memories of the past. Princess Nicholas was a frequent visitor and so, too, was Princess Marina.

During the early 1950s the writer Jennifer Ellis recalled having watched Marina

> ... helping an old lady who was trying to knit a pair of gloves and had got into difficulties. The Princess's sleek brown head was bent close to the white one; her face was set in concentration. But she was still young enough to be unable to hide the flicker of amusement in her eyes as she unravelled a thumb at least four times too big for any human hand.

The other home which most concerned Princess Nicholas was the one she herself established. If Dorothy Paget had taken pity on men and women who had known only privilege, Princess Nicholas's compassion drew no such distinction. Deeply disturbed that refugee children were left to fend for themselves while their parents took whatever work they could find, and haunted by scenes of orphans begging in the streets, Princess Nicholas acquired a large property at St-Germain-en-Laye. Under her supervision the house was soon functioning as a home and kindergarten, caring for sixty children ranging in age from two to twelve. Of the new residents, some could claim noble descent, while others were the children of ordinary men and women who had once been servants in imperial or well-to-do households. At Princess Nicholas's insistence, neither background nor class was to have any place at the home for, as she wisely pointed out, 'When they grow up they will have to work, so what is the use of starting them off with false ideas? And besides, children should never be made conscious of social differences.'

Twice a year Princess Nicholas would organize a ball, fête or bazaar to raise funds for her 'Home for Russian Children' and, in making arrangements for such events, she invariably enlisted the services of her daughters and their friends. Even the Nicholases' chauffeur and four servants were roped in to lend a helping hand. One room in the apartment was turned into an office and there mother, daughters and volunteers would spend long hours hard at work. Though most often a willing member of her mother's team, Marina made no secret of the fact that she much preferred being of practical assistance at the home itself. Strongly maternal, she was in her element when playing games with the older children, and at bathtime, when it came to getting the 'babies', as the two-, three- and four-year-olds were called, ready for bed.

Paris was a city for which Princess Marina always held a deep affection – and not without good reason for, had the Greek monarchy been more stable, the vitally important years of her youth and early womanhood would have been stifled by restrictive codes of protocol and convention. As it was, exile, despite some of its more obvious disadvantages, afforded Marina both the freedom and the anonymity in which to grow and develop as an individual unfettered by the cloistered atmosphere of court life.

Chapter Six

Toto and Prince George

Soon after she had completed her year at Princess Mestchersky's school in 1925, Princess Marina left Paris to visit her uncle Prince Christopher at his villa in Rome. After the death, in 1923, of his first wife Nancy, the Prince had decided to find a house in the city suitable for both himself and his mother, the dowager Queen Olga. His search ended when he found exactly what he was looking for in a villa owned by the Irish-born Baroness Aliotti. From that villa, with its 'sunny loggias, terraces and big garden', commanding a splendid view of Rome, Marina and her sister 'Woolly', as Princess Elizabeth had been nicknamed in childhood, were introduced by 'Uncle Christo' to the cream of Italian society. This Roman interlude marked the start of yet another round of travels for Princess Marina, one that was briefly interrupted by the death on 18 June 1926 of her seventy-five-year-old grandmother. Elderly though she was, Queen Olga appeared to enjoy good health, so that when her end came, it was doubly shocking to all her family save, perhaps, Prince Christopher himself.

In his memoirs, this obviously cultured and amusing man wrote of several psychic experiences he had had in his life. One such experience concerned the last days of his mother's life. In his book, the Prince tells us that his villa in Rome 'was built in the form of an L', which meant that he could see Queen Olga's wing from his own.

> I had returned from a party late one night, and on throwing back my shutters before getting into bed, I saw both her windows brilliantly illuminated. It was 2 am, and I wondered vaguely why she should be awake at that hour,

and then I noticed that the light was not like that from a night-light or an ordinary electric lamp. It was a golden glow that seemed to fill the whole room.

Next morning I asked her what she had been doing awake at that time of night, but she answered in surprise that she had never slept better in her life, and had not once turned on the light. I saw the strange light once more, and then left for Florence to stay with Queen Sophie, and forgot all about it. But one morning I awoke with an extraordinary premonition that I ought to leave for Rome. . . . I started immediately and arrived . . . to find my mother placidly having tea on the terrace with my sister. . . . But the next day my mother was taken ill, and in less than a week she had gone to join my father.

The night she died the golden glow was there again, a glorious golden light, full of promise of the reward to come.

Following her funeral service in Rome, Queen Olga's coffin was placed alongside that of her eldest son Constantine, in the crypt of the Russian church in Florence, where the red damask walls were hung with gold and silver icons, and the blue and white Greek flag decorated the ceiling. When, in due course, the Greek monarchy was restored once more, Queen Olga, King Constantine and, by then, Queen Sophie – who died in January 1932 – were to be accorded a triple state funeral in Athens, after which their bodies would be privately interred at Tatoi.

In the spring of 1927 Prince and Princess Paul again decided to spend the summer in England; and for the duration of their visit they rented Viscount Ednam's house in Cheyne Walk, Chelsea. Marina was invited to accompany her sister and brother-in-law, and at one point it almost looked as though she was about to win the heart of the Prince of Wales who, according to Neil Balfour, Prince Paul's biographer, 'appeared to take an unusual interest in her'. The Prince's attentions were apparently 'more than passing and went far beyond the call of duty and politeness. Paul was near certain and Marina completely overwhelmed, whilst Olga and her mother scarcely dared hope.'

Almost twenty-one, Princess Marina was now even more striking to look at than ever; she had developed the Parisienne's flair for fashion, while her air of polished sophistication loudly proclaimed her suitability as a possible Princess of Wales. The Greek word *porphyrogenitos* – 'born under the purple' – certainly summed up the dignity of Marina's bearing. But, despite all the excitement, the Prince of Wales lost interest and retreated to the security of his long-standing relationship with Freda Dudley-Ward – then still married to William Dudley Ward, Liberal Member of Parliament for Southampton, and whom he had first met at a party in London nine years earlier. How Princess Marina reacted to the heir apparent's curious behaviour is not clear. But if Princess Nicholas was disappointed that her youngest daughter no longer stood the ghost of a chance with the future King of England, she was to be equally miffed when her middle daughter failed to arouse so much as a flicker of interest in the future King of Italy.

Though Princess Nicholas, for all her pride in her impressive Romanov ancestry, cannot be said to have made a particularly prestigious marriage herself, she was never less than ambitious for her daughters. In short, she would have preferred each of them to have married kings. With her abortive engagement to Crown Prince Frederick, five years before, Olga had at least had the opportunity of one day becoming Queen of Denmark. Marina, had the relationship progressed further, might conceivably have bagged the Prince of Wales and, but for the fact that Princess Elizabeth was paraded too obviously in front of Crown Prince Umberto, it is not unreasonable to suppose that Princess Nicholas might have secured a consort's crown for at least one of her offspring.

In the meantime, while Princess Elizabeth and her matchmaking mother were staying with the Italian royal family at the Villa D'Este during the summer of 1928, Marina, Paul, and a heavily pregnant Olga were again in London. Arriving shortly before Olga's second confinement, Prince Paul, feeling like 'an old dowager chaperoning her grandchildren', escorted Marina to many of the social events which, for the fourth consecutive 'season', filled up her diary. *The* event for which both Prince and Princess Paul had waited so expectantly took place on 29 June, when Olga gave birth to her second son. At his christening a few weeks later, the infant prince was named Nicholas in honour of his grandfather.

With two grandchildren to his credit and a son-in-law whose

praises he couldn't sing loudly enough, the senior Prince Nicholas soon began teasing Marina and Elizabeth about their marital prospects. Despite the family's subtle – and not so subtle – attempts to find them acceptable husbands, they were both still single. Did they want to become old maids, Prince Nicholas asked? Neither princess rose to the bait. Instead, they simply assured their father, 'We don't want to get married yet.' Within five years both had changed their minds.

Not long after their own marriage, Prince and Princess Paul had been offered their very first home together, far away from the dull royal palace they shared with the King and Queen of Yugoslavia in Belgrade. Known as the Ermitage, this three-storey, timber chalet, which had been a royal shooting lodge, was situated at the top of the picturesque village of Bohinj Jezero, high in the Julian Alps. In what soon became something of a tradition, Olga's family spent part of every summer holiday at Bohinj for many years, enjoying the superlative beauty of the surrounding country-side and unwinding after their hectic activities in the capitals of Europe. In September 1933 there was scarcely any alteration to the established order at the Ermitage, save for the presence of a rather reserved thirty-three-year-old, with whom Paul and Olga, Marina and Elizabeth, had spent most of their time during a visit to Munich earlier that year.

'Toto' Toerring, or more formally, His Illustrious Highness Carl Theodor Klemens, Count zu Toerring-Jettenbach, a member of the famous Wittelsbach family, and a nephew of Queen Elizabeth of the Belgians, had been earmarked by Prince and Princess Paul as a possible husband for 'Woolly'. While they seemed to be quietly attracted to one another, Toto had given no definite indication of his feelings towards the least well known of Prince Nicholas's three daughters; hence his invitation to stay at Bohinj. Shortly after his arrival, Paul, Olga and Marina conveniently slipped away to London, leaving Toto and Woolly in the company of her parents and Uncle Christo, but otherwise quite alone. The ruse worked perfectly. On 22 September Toto finally proposed, and Elizabeth accepted. Four months later, on 10 January 1934, they were married in the chapel of Seefeld Castle, near Munich.

Of that close circle of girl cousins who had shared the game of 'Keeping House' on a Greek island many years before, only Marina, who was now twenty-seven, Irene, who was twenty-nine, and twenty-year-old Katherine remained unmarried. Olga and Elizabeth had found Paul and Toto; Princess Helen, though now divorced, had married Carol of Romania; while the four daughters of Prince Andrew, Margarita, Theodora, Cecile, and Sophie, had taken as their respective husbands, Gottfried, Eighth Prince of Hohenlohe-Langenburg; Berthold, Margrave of Baden; Georg Donatus, Hereditary Grand Duke of Hesse and by Rhine; and Prince Christoph of Hesse.

In his adulatory study of Princess Marina published in 1962, James Wentworth-Day alleged that, after the wedding of Princess Elizabeth and Count Toerring, an unidentified friend made the following observation of the bride's younger sister:

> The starry look in [Elizabeth's] eyes stirred something deep and, so far, unknown in Marina. From a lively, carefree girl she seemed to have suddenly grown into wistful womanhood. Her face acquired a new spiritual expression. She read more, she thought, perhaps she dreamt. This period of sudden spiritual growth was a vital one in her young life, and she herself must have been aware of it.
>
> I suddenly understood the change which had struck me in Princess Marina. I understood that the girl with those golden-brown eyes was a dreamer and a thinker. She was also an idealist; and she was hoping for these ideals and dreams to come true. I feel that she was capable of great feeling, and that the decisive moment had come for her.

All this, though it strikes one as far too poetic to be entirely believable, might have indicated some kind of 'spiritual' change in Marina at that time. Who can say? But it could also be argued – and far less romantically – that any single woman, the youngest among a family of closely united sisters, is very likely to experience deep emotions, perhaps even a period of introspection, when the last of her siblings marries and she is left alone.

Whatever Princess Marina may or may not have discovered about herself, following the marriage of Elizabeth and Toto, her own 'decisive moment' was soon to become manifest in the form of Prince George, fourth and youngest surviving son of King George v and Queen Mary. Like her parents and most of her relations, Marina was no stranger to the British royal family. But how well she herself actually knew any of them is open to question. 'I am sure we shall like Marina & that she will be a charming addition to the family', Queen Mary wrote to George v, when at last their youngest son became engaged. Yet even allowing for the fact that the Queen found it extremely difficult to communicate with other women, even those of her own family, this rather remote reference to the Princess who was, after all, her goddaughter, would tend to suggest that Marina was not on an intimate footing with members of the British royal house. Other early encounters with her royal kinsmen seemed to have been equally distant. The interest which the Prince of Wales had shown in Marina during her visit to London in 1927, for example, appeared to have developed remarkably suddenly, almost as if they had never met before. Nor is it certain that Prince George had ever been particularly aware of his future wife until the late summer of 1933.

That September, while Count Toerring was making up his mind about 'Woolly' at Bohinj, Marina accompanied Prince and Princess Paul to London. The chief purpose of their visit was to take their elder son Alexander back to school, though Paul never needed any excuse to find himself in England looking up old friends. Emerald Cunard, like the Duke and Duchess of York, and indeed Prince George himself, was just one such friend. Princess Marina met Prince George at a luncheon party that month given by the exotic Lady Cunard, one of London's leading hostesses. On that occasion the Princess and 'Georgie', as his family called him, established a rapport which led to several further meetings. Yet, by the time Marina left London with Olga and Paul at the end of that visit, there were no signs of a blossoming romance. On the contrary Prince George, who had quite a forceful personality of his own, declared that he found Marina too 'bossy'.

It is possible, of course, that this very bossiness was one of the traits George decided he liked in Marina. At all events, when she returned the following spring to stay with her sister and brother-in-law at Claridge's, Prince George was among the first to call. On the first of his many visits, however, bad timing meant that he had to while away several hours with Prince Paul – whom he had ostensibly dropped in to see – while Marina and Olga were out shopping. At length Princess Paul returned to the hotel, but without her sister. Marina, she explained, had gone on to the hairdressers. As the hours ticked by, it became abundantly clear that George had no other engagements that day, and was in no great hurry to leave. When at last Marina did appear, Prince George's delight was only too obvious, not only to the Princess herself but to Paul and Olga as well.

For the rest of her stay Marina and George lunched and dined together; went to the theatre and the cinema; danced at the Embassy Club in Bond Street; walked unnoticed in Green Park; visited the Prince of Wales at Fort Belvedere, his country house in Sunningdale; and went for long, fast, drives in George's sports car. Something had clicked and George was enchanted. 'She is the one woman with whom I could be happy to spend the rest of my life,' he said. 'We laugh at the same sort of thing. She beats me at most games and doesn't give a damn how fast I drive when I take her out in the car.'

Soon after, Princess Marina left London to join her mother at a health spa in Savoie in France, uncertain of when she and 'Georgie' would next see each other. Though Marina was not aware of it at the time, Prince Paul had already solved that mystery by inviting Prince George to stay at Bohinj that summer. And, of course, Marina would also be there.

Like Ascot and the Derby, Cowes week is one of the year's sporting highlights for the British royal family. But since Cowes equals boats rather than horses, fewer members of the royal family attend. In 1934, one sporting royal who did enjoy the sailing off the Isle of Wight was Prince George. It was then that he decided to cable Prince Paul to say that he would be arriving at Bohinj on 16 August. Almost as soon as Cowes week had ended George borrowed an aircraft from his brother David – the Prince of Wales had become the very first of Britain's royal pilots – and, without further ado, flew off in the direction of the Yugoslav airfield at Ljubljana, *en route* to Bohinj.

One member of the Greek royal family arrived at the 'Ermitage' one day ahead of Prince George. This was Marina's uncle Prince Christopher. As soon as Paul, Olga and Marina heard that George was about to join them, Prince Christopher received 'a mysterious SOS', telling him to 'get into the next train and come to Bohinj'. Fearing some catastrophe, the Prince immediately telephoned. Princess Olga answered and, in great excitement, explained the situation. 'Do you remember you were with us when Elizabeth got engaged to Toto?' she asked. 'They are both so happy that I have an idea you will bring Marina luck too.'

Though it has often been quoted in the years since his memoirs were first published in 1938, no biography of Princess Marina would be complete without Prince Christopher's commentary on what happened at Bohinj. This, in part, is what he wrote:

> . . . Prince George and his equerry Major [Humphrey] Butler
> arrived by air. . . . It was the first time I had seen George
> for some years and I was struck with his resemblance to his
> father at his age. He had the same habit of crinkling up his
> eyes when he smiled; his laugh was abolutely the King's.
>
> The weather was glorious and we spent the next few days
> in shooting, fishing, rambling through the woods and
> motoring over to luncheon or tea with my brother Nicholas
> and his wife, who had taken a villa twenty-five miles away.
> The atmosphere grew more and more electric.
>
> Then one evening we all played backgammon in the
> sitting-room until we could hardly keep awake. One by one
> we departed for bed until George and Marina were left
> sitting alone at opposite ends of the sofa.
>
> I had been in my bedroom for about half an hour when
> I discovered that I had left my cigarette-case on the
> backgammon table. Putting on my dressing-gown I went in
> search of it.
>
> The door of the sitting-room was open; George and
> Marina were still seated on the sofa, though no longer, I
> observed with satisfaction, at the opposite ends of it. I stole
> back to bed without my case.

Next day the Prince and Princess announced their engagement to Marina's family; though until King George v responded to his son's message seeking formal consent to the marriage, the couple's news had to remain a secret. To those unfamiliar with the protocol observed on such occasions, it may seem absurd that a grown man needed his father's approval before announcing to the world that he intended to get married. In Britain, however, any member of the royal family wishing to marry must first obtain the consent of the sovereign, under the terms of the Royal Marriages Act of 1772. The rules still apply today.

Despite all the red tape George v and Queen Mary were

delighted by their son's news and, on the evening of Tuesday 28 August, a statement was issued from Balmoral Castle which read: 'It is with the greatest pleasure that the King and Queen announce the betrothal of their dearly beloved son the Prince George to the Princess Marina, daughter of the Prince and Princess Nicholas of Greece, to which union the King has gladly given his consent.'

Chapter Seven

A King's Son

Prince George of Wales, as he was first known, was born at Sandringham on 20 December 1902. Thus, unlike his three elder brothers, all of whom were born during the reign of Queen Victoria, Prince George was an Edwardian. His grandfather, King Edward VII, was about to enter the third year of his reign at the time of Georgie's birth.

In retrospect, the image of Prince George as an Edwardian seems somehow to suit him very well. For the era which had taken his grandfather's name was not only an era of change, but one of romance, too. There was a new air of freedom and lightheartedness after the repressively sombre mood that epitomizes the age of Victoria. The difference in epoch also underlines the difference between Prince George and his brothers. For while he was to become a man very much of his time, the elder princes – save the future Duke of Windsor, in whom rebellion seems to have been present from the start – never entirely shook off the dust of their Victorian upbringing.

York Cottage, the birthplace of Prince George, was originally known as the Bachelor's Cottage. It stands to this day on the edge of the 'Lower Pond' – one of two such artificial features – in the grounds of Sandringham House, near King's Lynn in Norfolk, 120 miles north-east of London. Built by Edward VII when he was Prince of Wales, to accommodate some of the numerous guests attending the royal house parties, this relatively small Victorian lodge was given to Prince George's father, then Duke of York, as a wedding present, and appropriately renamed in his honour.

Stuffed with heavy 'modern' furniture from the fashionable firm

of Maple's, overheated in winter, suffocating in summer, and per-
meated by cooking smells whatever the season, York Cottage was
for thirty-three years the favourite residence of the Duke and
Duchess of York, even after they became King George V and Queen
Mary. As unattractive as it was ill-proportioned for the size of
family who would eventually live there, the house contained a
small entrance hall, the Duke of York's study or 'library', two
medium-sized drawing rooms, a dining room, and billiard room.
The Duke and Duchess each had a bedroom and dressing room
on the first, and only upper, floor; two or three further rooms
were set aside for members of the household, such as equerries
and ladies-in-waiting while, tucked away behind a swing door,
were the day nursery and the night nursery. In the latter the
York children all had their beds, as did their benevolent nanny,
Mrs 'Lala' Bill.

Georgie's father, a grandson of Queen Victoria, was Prince
George, second son of Edward and Alexandra, Prince and Princess
of Wales, afterwards King Edward VII and Queen Alexandra. His
mother was Princess Victoria Mary of Teck, known as 'May', only
daughter of Francis, Duke of Teck and Princess Mary Adelaide
of Cambridge. On 3 December 1891 Princess May became engaged
to Albert Victor, Duke of Clarence and Avondale and Earl of Athlone, known as 'Eddy', elder son of Edward and Alexandra and,
at that time, heir presumptive to the throne. As a boy Eddy had
been apathetic and backward. At home his gentleness had irritated
his father as much as it had endeared him to his mother, known
to her children as 'Motherdear'.

Of his royal heritage the Duke of Clarence knew little and cared
even less, preferring some rather shady forms of entertainment
to any function of an official nature. To quote James Pope-Hen-
nessy, Queen Mary's official biographer, 'Among the few things
Prince Eddy really cared for was every form of dissipation and
amusement.' Marriage, as was so often the case in those days,
seemed to be the only answer, and May of Teck, though shy
and reserved, was looked upon as the most suitable bride for
this dissolute young man. The wedding of Eddy and May was
arranged to take place on 27 February 1892 but, only six weeks
before that date, the bridegroom was taken ill. Influenza led to
inflammation of the lungs, and on 14 January he died.

For Princess May, the prospect of marrying the Duke of Clarence may not have been one of ecstasy, but fate and the royal family saw her as the future Queen of England and Eddy's younger brother George, by now Duke of York, was encouraged to think in terms of taking her as his own wife. Within sixteen months thought had been translated into deed. On 3 May 1893 Princess May kept an appointment for tea at the home of Princess Louise, Duchess of Fife, in Sheen, near Richmond. On her arrival she found that the Duke of York was also visiting his sister. That afternoon, Princess Louise helped matters along when she suggested, 'Now Georgie, don't you think you ought to take May into the garden to look at the frogs in the pond?'

'We walked together . . . in the garden,' May noted in her diary that evening, 'and he proposed to me, & I accepted him. Louise and MacDuff [the Duke of Fife] were delighted. I drove home to announce the news to Mama and Papa & Georgie followed . . . . We telegraphed to all the relations.'

Two months later, on 6 July, Prince George and Princess May were married in the Chapel Royal at St James's Palace. To Queen Victoria who sat, draped in lace and fanning herself, near the altar on that sultry afternoon, the Chapel Royal, even though it was where she and her 'Dearest Albert' were married in February 1840, was 'small & *very* ugly'. St George's Chapel at Windsor Castle, she declared, 'is lovely for a marriage in summer'.

With the most remarkable lack of taste and sensitivity, Prince George took his bride to honeymoon at York Cottage, Sandringham, the very house in which the Duke of Clarence had died a year and a half before, and where all his belongings were still to be found. 'All is left just as it was,' noted the Duke's aunt Vicky, the Empress Frederick of Germany, 'his dressing table and his watch, his brushes and combs and everything. His bed covered with a Union Jack in silk, and his photos and trifles and clothes, etc., in a glass cupboard.' For a honeymoon Queen Victoria considered the macabre setting of York Cottage 'rather *unlucky* and sad', and so, indeed, must many others. But such was the limited scope of the Duke of York's imagination.

Like Queen Victoria, May, Duchess of York, found childbirth and everything about it distasteful. By the end of the century, however, she had given her husband three children: Edward, or 'David', born shortly before his parents' first wedding anniversary, on 23 June 1894; Albert, otherwise 'Bertie', born on 14

December 1895; and Victoria, who was always known as Mary, the last of her four Christian names, born on 25 April 1897. Three more children followed: Prince Henry, or 'Harry', the Yorks' third son, was born on 31 March 1900, and Prince George on 20 December 1902. The couple's sixth and last child was Prince John. Born on 12 July 1905, this prince was discovered to suffer from epilepsy and, as was so often the case with Victorian and Edwardian society, the child was segregated from the rest of his family. Prince John was given a small household of his own at Wood Farm, on the Sandringham estate, and there, out of sight if not out of mind, he lived quietly until his early death on 18 January 1919, at the age of thirteen and a half.

With the sole exception of Prince Edward ('David'), who was born at White Lodge, Richmond, the Duchess of York gave birth to each of her children at York Cottage, around which so many of their youthful memories were to revolve. In later years, whenever the four princes and their sister recalled their childhood, Sandringham always stood out in sharp focus, as indeed did Edward VII and Queen Alexandra, their indulgent grandparents who lived at the 'Big House' – as they called Sandringham House itself – a quarter of a mile away through the park.

David, Bertie and Mary were all educated privately at York Cottage, before the elder boys were sent off to the Royal Naval Colleges at Osborne and Dartmouth. Prince George and his brother Harry were also taught privately at first. Then Harry was sent to Eton, while his younger brother went off to St Peter's School at Broadstairs, on the south coast. At the time of George's engagement to Princess Marina, the Marquess of Donegall, a fellow pupil at St Peter's, recalled one particularly human impression of the schoolboy prince. In the *Sunday Dispatch* of 2 September 1934 he wrote:

> In those days Prince George, in contrast to his well-groomed appearance of later years, had an obstinate tuft of hair on the top of his head which refused to obey brush or comb. When more than usually puzzled over how long it would take A, B, and C to do the traditional 'piece of work', he would curl the recalcitrant tuft with the index finger of his left hand. This appeared to produce the required inspiration.

Of the four royal brothers, Prince George was academically the brightest. School reports from Mr A.J.Richardson, Headmaster of St Peter's, were so gratifying that the Prince's parents went in person to thank him. 'But, sir', said Richardson, 'Prince George applies himself to every subject. It is a joy to teach such a child.' The same could not be said, however, of either David or Bertie. Though far from stupid, both were repeatedly admonished for their lack of application and bad exam results; while the unfortunate Prince Henry, afterwards Duke of Gloucester, was never anything more than bovine. 'Do for goodness sake wake up and work harder and use the brains God has given you,' wrote Harry's exasperated mother when he was still at Eton. 'All you write about is your everlasting football of which I am heartily sick.'

In November 1901, ten months after Edward VII's accession to the throne, George, Duke of York was created Prince of Wales, the title traditionally held by the heir apparent. But unlike his father, on whom the title was bestowed one month after his birth in 1841, and was borne by him for almost sixty years, Prince George was to be king-in-waiting for less than a decade. On 6 May 1910 Edward VII died, six months short of his sixty-ninth birthday.

The coronation of King George V and Queen Mary (as 'Georgie' and 'May' had now become) took place at Westminster Abbey on 22 June the following year. Witnessing the epic ritual from the front row of the royal gallery, were four of their children, Mary, Bertie, Harry and George. David had by now succeeded his father as the twentieth Prince of Wales, and as such, was required to take part in the ceremony itself. While the princes had behaved impeccably in the Abbey, all hell broke loose during the return procession to Buckingham Palace. The diarist Lord Crawford wrote:

> One of the great successes of the Coronation was a standup fight between the two kilted princes [George and Harry, then aged nine and eleven] after the ceremony. . . . By some imprudence the Prince of Wales and his sister were sent in a state coach with the younger brothers but without a controlling prelate or pedagogue. When fairly started from the Abbey, a free fight began to the huge delight of the spectators in Whitehall. The efforts of Princess Mary to mollify the combatants were sincere but ineffectual, and during the strife she nearly had her sweet little coronet

knocked off! Peace was ultimately restored after about fifty yards of hullaballoo.

During that summer of 1911 the people of Great Britain, indeed of the Empire as a whole, were served a double helping of royal ceremonial. For at Caernarvon Castle on 14 July, just three weeks after his parents' coronation, David was formally invested as Prince of Wales and Earl of Chester. It was the closest he would ever come to a coronation of his own. At this time, David was into his second year at Dartmouth as a naval cadet. While the meaning of his Investiture and the necessity of such an occasion was quite clear to him, certain other aspects of the show caused embarrassment. Chief among them was his costume of satin, velvet and ermine, which – and not without reason – he disdainfully referred to as 'this preposterous rig'. Throughout his career as heir apparent, and even when he occupied the throne in 1936 as King Edward VIII, David was always among the most democratic of princes; one of the reasons why, as he admitted in a television interview forty years after his abdication, his clash with the British Establishment had been 'inevitable'.

Though Prince George was never to offer a direct challenge to the established view of the monarchy, he was every bit as democratic as his brother, and just as much an individual. There were, of course, notable differences in their characters, but even so they were alike in many respects. They shared the same sense of humour, the same energy and the same passion for keeping fit. They had very similar tastes in music, adored night life, and sometimes formed relationships that were not always considered 'acceptable'. In his brother David also found a kind of mentor; one to whom he could unburden his soul in complete trust and confidence. In *A King's Story*, David, by then the Duke of Windsor, wrote: 'Although George was eight and a half years my junior, I found in his character qualities that were akin to my own ... we became more than brothers – we became close friends.'

Not long before his fourteenth birthday in 1916, Prince George embarked on what was arguably the unhappiest period of his life. Right from the start he was aghast at the thought of having to follow David and Bertie into the Royal Navy, first at Osborne, then Dartmouth. Life as a naval cadet would not, in a million years, have been George's personal choice. James Wentworth-Day even claimed that the Prince's fondness for wearing a kilt had led him to hope that he might be allowed to join the Army in a Highland regiment. Whatever the truth of the matter, George's immediate future had been settled for him by the Lord High Admiral in person; in other words, his father the King. In an attempt to dissuade her husband from sending Georgie to naval college, Queen Mary tried to make the King understand that it might do the boy more harm than good. It was unusual for the Queen to intercede on her children's behalf at any time since, as she said herself, she had always to remember that their father was also their King. But in this instance she made an exception. Of all her offspring, Queen Mary saw much of herself mirrored in Prince George, not least in their mutual appreciation of the arts. Though it is extremely doubtful whether Queen Mary ever really tried to understand her children, she was the first to realize the error of sending this particular son into an environment that his sensitive and artistic temperament would find completely alien.

When writing of his brother many years later, the Duke of Windsor was to make specific mention of some of Prince George's finer qualities. 'Possessed of unusual charm of manner and a quick sense of humour and talented in many directions, he had an undoubted flair for the arts,' the Duke wrote. 'He played the piano, knew a good deal about music, and had a knowledgeable eye for antiques.' All this in a young man would not normally point to the armed forces as a place to be. But while Queen Mary and her eldest son appreciated that fact, the King himself would not be moved. An aesthete Prince George might be, but a sailor he would become. On that note, the Prince was packed off to the junior naval college at Osborne on the Isle of Wight. At least to begin with, he seemed to settle in, applying himself dutifully to his studies and achieving far higher grades than either David or Bertie. Then, through boredom or unhappiness, perhaps both, Prince George's concentration waned and, from the top of the scholastic ladder, he began slipping towards the bottom – from where, incidentally, his brothers in their time had never advanced. Languages were to prove George's saving grace, however. Four years after leaving the senior naval academy at Dartmouth in Devon, he attended a course at the Royal Naval College in Green-wich. There he gained first place in French and second place in

Italian in the voluntary examination in foreign languages for Acting Sub-Lieutenants. Later still, his proficiency was further acknowledged, when his duties started to include those of interpreter in French.

Yet whatever services Prince George was able to render the Navy, the Navy was to disrupt his health. Sea-sickness and insomnia plagued him from the start of his first voyage and, in 1929, were greatly to contribute to his being relieved of the career so ruthlessly imposed on him. In the interim George had no choice but to make the most of a disagreeable situation. In April 1920, at the age of seventeen, he passed out of Dartmouth, and nine months later, newly promoted to the rank of midshipman, he was detailed to HMS *Iron Duke*, flagship of the Mediterranean fleet. Service aboard HMS *Queen Elizabeth* and the flotilla leader HMS *Mackay* then followed and, with subsequent promotion, he was appointed in turn to HMS *Hawkins*, the flagship in China; HMS *Nelson*, flagship of the Home Fleet; and HMS *Durban*.

Though Prince George's service career caused him untold regrets, life was not without its compensations. Nor, indeed, did 'PG', or 'Babe' as he was known, ever lose his sense of humour. In her book *Princess Marina: Her Life and Times* Stella King wrote:

> Once in China, some press cameramen, hearing that British
> royalty was about, met him when he was about to board
> his ship and asked if he had seen the 'King of England'.
> Without hesitation he gestured behind him towards the
> ship's doctor, a heavily-built man who was being carried in
> a sedan chair, and left them to sort it out for themselves.
> He laughed a great deal when the portly doctor's picture
> appeared in a newspaper later with a caption saying that
> he was the 'English King'.

Despite such amusing incidents, the undisputed rewards of visiting far-flung places, and the entertaining companionship of his compatriots, Prince George continued to petition his father for permission to leave the Navy. The King would have none of it; but George refused to let go of the hope that he might be allowed to do something more constructive with his life. By 1928, that ambition was closer to being fulfilled than the Prince realized.

During Ascot week that year Mabell, Countess of Airlie, who had frequently acted as sounding-board and confessor to the children of her old friend Queen Mary, was staying at Windsor Castle in her capacity as lady-in-waiting; a post she had held ever since 'May' became Princess of Wales. At dinner one evening, the dowager Countess was seated next to Prince George, who told her how much he was dreading his next voyage. Lady Airlie recalled in her memoirs some thirty years later:

> He was not happy in the Navy and wanted to go into the Civil Service or the Foreign Office, but the King would not hear of it.
>
> 'His only reason for refusing is that it has never been done before,' the Prince said. 'I've tried to make him see that I'm not cut out for the Navy, but it's no use. What can I do?'
>
> I advised him not to waste time in arguing with the King – which would only make him angry – but to work hard while he was at sea, get the Civil Service papers and do them, and then let his father see the results. He told me some time later that he had acted on my advice, and that it had been successful.

The King's change of heart was not due solely to the results of his son's Civil Service exams, but rather to medical reports which made it clear that Prince George's digestive trouble would severely undermine his health, were he to be forced to continue in the Navy. A year later George was promoted to the rank of Commander and, to his profound relief, finally discharged from the service.

For the next three years the King's son – the first prince ever to have become a civil servant – was attached to the Foreign Office. His duties there, however, did not prove sufficiently demanding. Like the Prince of Wales, George had developed an enormous liking for the working man. And like David, he not only became interested in social and industrial conditions, but shared his brother's deep concern for the misery of the unemployed who, by 1931, totalled more than two million. It was this very real social conscience, formed largely through his experiences in the Navy, that led Prince George to change departments within the Civil Service. From his desk at the Foreign Office, overlooking St James's Park, he moved along Whitehall to the Home Office. This move, arranged by Sir Herbert Samuel, the Home Secretary, and Sir Malcolm Delevigne, Permanent Under-Secretary of State, resulted in

George becoming a Home Office Factory Inspector. In his initial report to Sir Herbert, Delevigne itemized the scope of the Prince's duties, notwithstanding the King's instruction that his son should remain available for royal engagements as and when required. He wrote:

> As his work will lie in the Metropolitan area we would propose to attach him to three London districts, Southwark, Woolwich and South Essex, in order to give him as interesting a range of work as possible and at the same time allow of some concentration of interest in the more important and live issues of factory administration. . . . Among the more important and live issues to which his attention might be given are the work in the London docks (loading and unloading of ships, which are processes fruitful of accident and are governed by an elaborate code of regulations, and which happen to be, at the moment, the subject of international discussion); the asbestos industry with its newly discovered dangers to health; different branches of the engineering and woodworking industries; the building industry with its recently amended code of safety regulations, etc. It would also be arranged to let him see interesting developments in health and welfare work. . . .
> . . . the actual visiting of the factories should be alternated with visits to the Home Office Industrial Museum . . . where he would be given some intensive instruction in the principles and practice of the safeguarding of machinery and the prevention of various kinds of accidents; the nature and prevention of industrial diseases and the promotion of industrial health and welfare; the principles of factory ventilation and lights; and so on. This is now part of the ordinary training of recruits to the Factory Inspectorate.

With the full approval of both the King and the Prime Minister, Stanley Baldwin, Prince George joined the Home Office on 12 April 1932. From the start George took to his new occupation as if born to it. In many respects, the Prince's work complemented that of another of his brothers. Motivated by a similar wish to be of practical benefit to the ordinary man, Prince Albert, Duke of York ('Bertie'), had already become involved with industry under the auspices of the Industrial Welfare Association, of which he was president. The overall aim of this organization was to entice Britain's industrial overlords to become more actively conscious of the need to improve working conditions for employees, to establish health centres and factory canteens, and to provide recreation facilities.

As Sir John Wheeler-Bennett, Bertie's official biographer, was to put it, 'Captains of Industry and Trade Union leaders became regular callers [on the Duke of York] . . . and the Duke's influence made itself felt throughout the industrial life of Britain.' Between them, 'the Foreman' and the 'Factory Inspector', as Bertie and George were respectively nicknamed by members of their family, proved that royalty could serve more than a purely decorative function. Indeed, it could be argued that no princes, before or since, have ever achieved more in helping to better the conditions of Britain's workforce.

In his work for the Home Office Prince George proved to be a popular and conscientious member of the Factory Inspectorate. Even more to the point, he was of value both to his department and to those whose working conditions it was his responsibility to review. Like his brother Bertie, Prince George insisted that he should be allowed to do his job without ceremony. Employers were never to be given advance warning of his identity, lest factories should be smartened up and unwanted reception committees organized. In short, if his work was to be effective, George wanted to do it as anonymously as the rest of his Home Office colleagues. For the most part, that is exactly how it was; but it would have been ridiculous of anyone to have suggested that the Prince was never recognized. It stands to reason that, on occasion, he was. Yet, more than fifty years ago, when media technology was more primitive, and public interest in the royal family was by no means as manic or intrusive as it is today, princes were in a far better position to move about unnoticed and unmolested.

In an official capacity, of course, the very opposite was true. If the Prince of Wales, by far the best-looking and most charismatic of George v's sons, was adored by millions as a royal matinée idol, Prince George ran a close second. Physically the younger man was somewhat taller than David, and dark where his brother was fair. Both had blue eyes, though George's were a deeper shade; and where David's voice was comparatively strong, with a slight inflection often likened to Cockney, George's gentler voice was best described as whimsical. Towards the end of his life David's features, in certain moods, tended to assume the unmistakable look of his Hanoverian ancestors, whereas Prince George, particularly in the set of his eyes and mouth, *always* closely resembled the court portraits of England's earlier Georges; none more so, in fact, than Jean-Étienne Liotard's famous painting of the young King George III.

After Prince George left the Navy, he and the Prince of Wales moved even closer together, in the sense that they now lived under the same roof. David had never liked Buckingham Palace, and during the mid-1920s had been delighted when his father agreed to his setting up home at York House, St James's Palace. Once the official London residence of George V and Queen Mary themselves, and now, coincidentally, the home of the present Duke and Duchess of Kent, York House forms part of the rambling red-brick Tudor palace on the Mall which Henry VIII had built for his second queen, Anne Boleyn. It stands on the site of the hospital of St James the Less, a home for leprous maidens; and even to this day, some of the flagstones, incised with a faded cross, mark the graves of some of the victims.

Having George share his house, away from the censorious eye of their father, was a great pleasure to the Prince of Wales, and between them they lived life to the full. David, fond of flying, steeplechasing, hunting, shooting and golf, was as much at home in the company of sportsmen, as he was in London's most fashionable night clubs, perfecting the latest dances with his successive lady-loves, Mrs Dudley Ward, Thelma Lady Furness, and latterly the vivacious American whom the entire western hemisphere would soon know as Mrs Simpson. Prince George shared his brother's fondness for flying, but not for shooting. George preferred to go sailing or skiing. His love of nightlife, however, was certainly as legendary as that of the Prince of Wales, as was his fondness for high-spirited pranks.

The jazz musician Tiny Winters, who often saw the princes together at the Embassy Club, recalled one occasion when they stayed on all night. The moment they left, said Winters, the band 'shot out to catch the buses', and as they did so, ran into the royal brothers, who had 'just got out into the street, and one of them got [the other's] top hat and climbed up a lamp-post and stuck [it] on the iron bar. . . . Then the other one climbed up and got it. After that they were chasing one another, grabbing their top hats and kicking them about all over the street.'

In his quest for a good time, some of Prince George's other activities were not so innocent. At the end of the 1920s, for example, one of Prince George's lovers, Kiki Whitney Preston, an American beauty who was part of Kenya's Happy Valley set – the subject of James Fox's book *White Mischief* – introduced the Prince to cocaine and morphine. It was an addiction from which George helped by his brother David, who installed him in a quiet country house with qualified nursing staff, took some time to recover. Then as now, the high-born, with time on their hands and money to throw away, were among those who thought little of experiment ing with fashionable drugs. But that he should have been one of them revealed an unfortunate weakness in George's character.

Another of the Prince's weaknesses was his passion for sex. As much with men as with women, with aristocrats, show business personalities or with strangers, George's appetite for sexual adventure was voracious. His taste in women, both before and after his marriage, was catholic, recognizing no boundaries either in race or colour. Indeed, black women greatly appealed to him, and among his earliest mistresses was Florence Mills, an American entertainer whom the Prince had first met in London during the run of *Blackbirds*, one of Charles B. Cochran's reviews. A further entanglement of much greater intensity, was George's passion for Poppy Baring, a fun-loving young débutante. The diplomat and author Duff Cooper, later Viscount Norwich, watched closely. On 8 January 1927 he found 'Poppy sleeping peacefully in the arms of Prince George'. Six days later, he noted that there was 'talk of marriage', although Poppy herself said 'she couldn't bear the Royal Family'. At the end of the month, George, with his customary love of speed, dashed off to tell his parents that he wanted to marry. According to Duff Cooper, the King and Queen took it 'wonderfully and raised hardly any objection. . . .' Ten days later, however, it was all off. 'Unfavourable reports about poor Poppy appear to have reached His Majesty's ears . . . so the girl's sunk.' Of his homosexual lovers Noël Coward, then in his mid-twenties, was undoubtedly among the most famous. In later life the 'Master', as this multi-talented man was known within the theatre world, described his relationship with Prince George as 'a little dalliance', though Charles Russell, Coward's New York representative, told the author Michael Thornton that 'Noël used to refer constantly to his affair with the Duke of Kent. He seemed rather proud of it and at times was almost a bore on the subject.'

During the 1920s and '30s Noël Coward not only became a close friend of Prince George but also established a warm friendship with Princess Marina that would last for the rest of her life. In fact, they became so close after Prince George's death that the Marquess of Carisbrooke jokingly told Coward, 'You know, of course, Noël, that you can never be Dowager Duke of Kent.'

In satisfying his homosexual tendencies, the Prince's taste in men was no less eclectic than his taste in women, though George, whom Prince Louis Ferdinand of Prussia found to be 'artistic and effeminate and used a strong perfume', did have a particular penchant for the blond good looks of German boys. Yet if the Prince was discreet in most of his relationships, there was one episode in 1932, when, according to Sir Robert Bruce Lockhart, diplomat and journalist, there was 'a scandal about Prince George – letters to a young man in Paris. A large sum had to be paid for their recovery.'

At that time, as her own relationship with the Prince of Wales gathered momentum, Wallis Simpson was among those who saw a great deal of Prince George, both in London and at Fort Belvedere in Sunningdale, David's superb country retreat six miles from Windsor. In her memoirs Wallis, by then Duchess of Windsor, tactfully referred to David's concern for his brother, when she wrote, 'I had a distinct feeling, as I watched them together, that the older brother was at times a little worried, even anxious, about the younger, perhaps, because he was too lighthearted.'

Besides the sex, drugs and games that all but dominated Prince George's private life, there was also that aspect of his character, touched upon earlier, that cared deeply about things of beauty, ranging from priceless works of art to interior decoration. As a bachelor prince, he received a Civil List allowance of £10,000 a year until he married. Then his tax-free income was raised to £25,000 per annum; the equivalent of far more than £100,000 today. Yet even on an annuity of £10,000, George accumulated a very fine collection of antique furniture, first-edition books, Georgian silver, porcelain, bibelots and pictures, including, as Kenneth Rose noted in *Kings, Queens and Courtiers*, 'the Altieri Claudes, brought to England by Nelson'. Of Prince George's prowess as a collector, Sir Oliver Millar, the present Keeper of the Queen's Pictures, has said that he was 'the most distinguished royal connoisseur since George IV'.

Such then was the measure of the man whose proposal Princess Marina accepted one evening in August 1934, while staying with her sister and brother-in-law at their lodge high in the Slovenian mountains. Whilst she certainly appreciated George's finer points, no one can be sure how much this perceptive and not unworldly young woman knew of his peccadilloes before or after their marriage.

Chapter Eight

Duke and Duchess of Kent

Until news of her engagement to Prince George was announced, Princess Marina was an unknown quantity. Royalty in exile rarely excite attention, and the Greek royal family was no exception. Yet when Prince and Princess Nicholas accompanied their daughter and her fiancé back to Paris from Bohinj, Marina was no longer the unknown princess who (like many aristocratic women of modest means) had posed for publicity photographs to promote Pond's Cold Cream, had strolled in the Bois de Boulogne, fed the swans in the Tuileries Gardens or travelled around the city by public transport.

Suddenly, or so it seemed, everybody in Paris knew who she was and, just as suddenly, friends who had deserted the family when they were expelled from Greece sprang up from nowhere to offer congratulations in the hope of rejoining Prince and Princess Nicholas's diminished circle. At the Gare du Nord, upon their arrival from Yugoslavia, the royal party was besieged by crowds anxious to catch a glimpse of the Prince and Princess; while British and European reporters, barely restrained by a cordon of gendarmes, jostled with each other for stories and photographs. Astounded though they were by such an unexpected welcome, Prince Nicholas is alleged to have been indignant at the sudden acknowledgement of his family's existence. 'Darling, what *does* it matter?' Marina is said to have asked her father. 'Would you expect people to behave otherwise?'

Within the next few weeks the British public knew all there was to know about Prince George's fiancée, from carefully prepared notes released to the press, newspaper features and cinema newsreels. Even the Princess herself yielded to media blandishments and gave interviews in her parents' apartment. During the 1930s, half a century before government health warnings, national no-smoking days and the like, the sight of public figures with lighted cigarettes in their hands caused scant comment. Yet, because she was a princess, Marina caused a minor stir when she was first seen smoking in public. The Duke of Windsor once summed up that kind of reaction, when he said, 'It has been my experience that the pleased incredulity with which the public reacts to the elementary demonstrations on the part of royalty that they are, after all, like other people, is matched by the public's firm refusal to accept them as such.'

On 12 September, leaving Marina in Paris to consult Edward Molyneux, the famous British-born couturier, about her wedding dress and trousseau, Prince George flew back to London. That same afternoon, before preparing to take the night train to Scotland – his sleeping compartment had been reserved in the name of 'Mr Smith' – the Prince selected the ring he would give to his bride-to-be. His choice was a square Kashmir sapphire, flanked by baton (oblong) diamonds and set in platinum. Princess Marina invariably wore her engagement ring, and later her plain gold wedding band, on the third finger of her right hand, in accordance with the custom in Greece, and indeed in many other countries.

Three days later, on Saturday 15 September, Prince George left Balmoral Castle, where he had joined the King and Queen, to travel back to York House. The following day Marina and her parents arrived at Folkestone from France. The size of the crowds who waited to greet her, and the cheers of welcome, were later compared to the scenes which surrounded the arrival of her late great-aunt Alexandra of Denmark, 'the Sea-King's daughter', seventy-one years earlier. Feeling 'a little dazed', as she put it, Marina told reporters, 'I am so overwhelmed. I had not expected this wonderfully generous reception.' Folkestone's generosity was equalled at London's Victoria Station, where Prince George greeted his fiancée. Outside thousands gathered in the streets for a glimpse of the Princess and, in a spontaneous gesture of goodwill, women threw handfuls of rose petals in front of the royal car as it slowly made its way towards St James's Palace. There yet another crowd waited, though this one, reluctant to disperse once the couple had stepped inside York House, soon began calling for them. In response to cries of 'We want Marina', the Prince and Princess appeared at an open window. As she waved, Marina's engagement ring caught the light, and a voice from the crowd shouted, 'What stone is it?'

'It's a sapphire,' the Princess called back, moving her hand from side to side.

A few weeks later Prince George wrote to his old friend – and Marina's brother-in-law – Prince Paul of Yugoslavia, to thank him 'a million times' for his hospitality at Bohinj and 'for letting me see Marina and so get engaged to her'. The Prince enthused,

> It's all so lovely and I am so happy that I can hardly believe it. Everyone is so delighted with her – the crowd especially – 'cos when she arrived at Victoria Station they expected a dowdy princess – such as unfortunately my family are – but when they saw this lovely chic creature – they could hardly believe it and even the men were interested and shouted 'Don't change – don't let them change you!' Of course she won't be changed – not if I have anything to do with it.
> My parents were charming and so pleased with M. and me!

From the 1850s the royal family has traditionally spent August, September and early October on holiday at Balmoral in the Scottish Highlands. It was from there that George v and Queen Mary had announced their son's engagement, and it was there that Princess Marina, together with Prince and Princess Nicholas, spent the week that followed their arrival in Britain. As traditional as the royal family's annual pilgrimage to the Deeside estate which Queen Victoria called 'this Dear Paradise', was – and still is – the ghillies' ball.

That summer it was held in the spartan ballroom of Balmoral Castle on the evening of 19 September. Preceded by seven pipers, the King and Queen led Prince George and Princess Marina, the Duke and Duchess of York, and Prince and Princess Arthur of Connaught down the oak staircase to the recessed royal daïs. There the King – who no longer danced – settled himself next to the Archbishop of Canterbury, Dr Cosmo Gordon Lang, to watch the festivities. The programme that night, as at every ghillies' ball since 1919, featured twelve dances; among them a Paul Jones, The Dashing White Sergeant, the Circassian Circle, Spanish Gavotte and Flirtation Polka. In honour of Princess Marina, who had taken lessons from Queen Mary, and danced every dance, a Greek national air was included in the selection of music. 'I was enchanted [by] the ghillies' ball,' Marina told friends afterwards. 'There the servants dance with the royal family without any sense of familiarity, but with the utmost good friendship.'

Two days later it was announced that the wedding of Prince George and Princess Marina would take place at Westminster Abbey on the morning of Thursday 29 November. The announcement added that, following the Anglican service, a second ceremony would take place, this time according to the rites of the Greek Orthodox Church, of which the Princess remained a lifelong member. *The Times* commented:

> A precedent for the holding of a second service at a royal
> marriage is provided by the wedding of the late Duke of
> Edinburgh [Prince Alfred, second son of Queen Victoria] . . .
> to the late Grand Duchess Marie Alexandrovna of Russia
> [second daughter of Tsar Alexander II] on January 23, 1874,
> in the Winter Palace at St Petersburg. On that occasion . . .
> the bride and bridegroom were first married according to
> the Greek [sic] rite in the Imperial Chapel, and again,
> immediately afterwards, in accordance with the Church of
> England service, read in the Alexander Hall by the Dean of
> Westminster (Dean Stanley) . . .

On 24 September Prince George and Princess Marina returned to London once more, again by overnight sleeper. Reaching King's Cross just before 7.30 that morning, the royal party looked out on a platform massed with men and women who, despite the hour, waited to cheer them. From the station George drove Marina to Claridge's, where she and her parents occupied one of the elegant suites on the second floor. The Prince then went home to York House, but not before arranging to have a box each of pink roses and of pink lilies delivered to his fiancée.

Shortly after midday, George was back at the hotel to lunch with Marina, her parents and the Infanta Beatrice of Spain, after which the Prince took his bride to visit Cartier the jewellers, to shop for personal gifts. Cartier was, in fact, one of Prince George's favourite haunts and when, four years later, he was appointed Governor-General designate of Australia, Chips Channon, diarist and MP, wryly commented that the Prince's posting 'would save him £500,000 or more, the money he would certainly have spent in London shops'.

In celebration of Prince George's marriage, and by way of personal tribute to his son, the King declared his intention of reviving a royal title that had fallen into abeyance with the death of Queen Victoria's father 114 years before. In April 1799 King George III, great-great-grandfather of George V, created his fourth son Edward Duke of Kent and Strathearn and Earl of Dublin. When the Duke died twenty-one years later, leaving his German widow with an eight-month-old daughter, the future Queen Victoria, his titles died with him. Now George V had decided to create that honour anew and, on 12 October 1934, Prince George became Duke of Kent, Earl of St Andrews and Baron Downpatrick.

By then Princess Marina had returned to Paris with her parents; but before they left, she issued a statement which, in many ways, encapsulates her essential humanity. The Princess said,

> I would like the people of England to share in some way
> my great happiness on the occasion of my engagement to
> Prince George. As you know, my years of exile have taught
> me how much unhappiness there is in the world. Although
> I should be happy to think that the preparations for my
> wedding were in some small measure giving employment
> to those who need it, I should be more than happy for the
> unemployed, and particularly for their children, to receive
> any money which has been intended for the purchase of
> wedding gifts for me.

Princess Marina's altruistic regard for the poor of Britain served to increase her popularity still further. Yet while many cities and towns did send wedding presents, others responded to the Princess's appeal and put official funds to more practical use.

Amid her family's happiness at Marina's approaching marriage, one event occurred that briefly threatened plans for the November wedding and subdued the pleasurable sense of anticipation among all those most directly concerned. On 9 October, less than an hour after he had stepped ashore in Marseilles at the start of a state visit to France, King Alexander of Yugoslavia was assassinated by a man who leaped onto the running board of the open-topped car in which he was travelling and shot the King at point-blank range. On the night before he set out for France, Princess

Paul – Marina's sister Olga – had urged Alexander to wear his bulletproof vest, but her pleas had been dismissed.

In his will the King appointed three men – Prince Paul, Alexander's cousin; Ivan Perović, Governor of Croatia; and Radenko Stanković, Professor of Medicine at Belgrade University, and a man who had won the monarch's confidence – to rule Yugoslavia as regents until his eleven-year-old son King Peter II attained his majority in September 1941. Of the three Prince Paul was nominated chief regent. The funeral of the murdered King took place in Belgrade on 14 October. Princess Marina was among the mourners, together with her husband-to-be, the new Duke of Kent, acting as the official representative of George V and the British people.

At home in England during the weeks that led up to the royal wedding the Prince of Wales nursed a personal sorrow of his own; the imminent loss of his favourite brother and intimate friend. The Duchess of Windsor later recalled:

> As I watched the Prince . . . it seemed to me that a sadness
> began to envelop him. He and his younger brother were
> very close, and the bonds of blood were strengthened by
> an unusual kinship of spirit. . . . Before his wedding, Prince
> George was at [Fort Belvedere] almost every weekend. I
> rather suspected that the Prince, who was to be best man
> . . . thought it was just as well to keep a close eye on the
> bridegroom-to-be until he had been safely led to the altar.

If, however, the Prince of Wales was to lose 'the only powerful male relationship he had ever known in his life', as Audrey Whiting put it in *The Kents*, he was about to win the most powerful relationship he was ever to know with a woman. That year, he and Wallis Simpson had taken a private holiday cruise aboard Lord Moyne's yacht *Rosaura*, and it was then, in Wallis's own words, that she and the Prince 'crossed the line that marks the indefinable boundary between friendship and love'.

For the time being, of course, the only love story all Europe was interested in was that of George and Marina, or 'that dazzling pair', as Chips Channon referred to them during the early years of their marriage. By the third week of November London was *en fête* and waiting only for the start of *the* royal event of 1934.

Princess Marina was back from Paris and, with Prince and Princess Nicholas, staying at Buckingham Palace as the guest of the King and Queen. There on 27 November a sumptuous pre-wedding ball for more than 2,000 guests was held in honour of the bridal couple, while in the West End vast crowds marvelled at the brilliance and ingenuity of the street decorations. Bond Street, in particular, had pulled out all the stops, and its entire length was hung with garlands of waxed-paper flowers, forming brightly coloured arches, from which were suspended hundreds of Greek and British flags. Wedding bells, entwined monograms, and portraits of the bride and bridegroom were inevitably displayed in nearly every shop window, while coloured lights and festive streamers heightened the carnival-like atmosphere. At St James's Palace the last of the exhibits were being put into position before the wedding presents went on public display in aid of charity. Among the gifts silver and furniture predominated. The Lord Mayor and Citizens of the City of London, for example, presented a magnificent silver dinner service; the Corporation of the City of London gave a set of eighteenth-century silver tureens and plate. The Prime Minister and the Cabinet gave a partner's desk in English walnut and British Honduras mahogany; the twelve senior Livery Companies presented a set of six Queen Anne walnut chairs. Other gifts were also chosen to appeal to the Duke's taste. The Royal Academy gave a George III bracket clock. The President of Czechoslovakia sent an unusual set of engraved glass; the President of France seven classical groups in Sèvres porcelain. More originally, the Greek community in Cape Town sent Princess Marina a huge fan of eighteen prime ostrich feathers mounted in mother-of-pearl. Shops patronized by the couple were also prominent, notably Messrs M. Harris & Son, who presented a superb antique red and gold lacquered cabinet on an immensely elaborate gilded stand, together with a six-panelled Chinese screen. Boucheron gave a jade and diamond cigarette box with jewelled clasp and hinges; Cartier gave a pigskin toilet case with silver-gilt mounts, specially designed for the Duke of Kent.

This random selection gives but a small indication of the range and volume of presents received by the royal couple, though many of those who visited the exhibition were more interested in the gifts presented to the Duke and his fiancée by members of the royal family themselves. The King and Queen gave early nineteenth-century silver candelabra, wine coolers and bread baskets. From the Prince of Wales the couple received a pair of Adam mahogany tables and a pair of hall stools; Princess Louise, Duchess of Argyll, the Duke of Connaught and Prince and Princess Arthur of Connaught gave an antique mirror; from Princess Victoria there was a black onyx cigarette box with a marcasite fastening. From the Princesses Elizabeth and Margaret and their cousins George and Gerald Lascelles came a pair of silver wine holders. From abroad, there was a fourfold screen from Queen Wilhelmina of the Netherlands, a silver cock and hen from the Emperor of Japan – symbolic of married happiness – while Prince and Princess Christopher of Greece gave a specially commissioned portrait of the bride's mother Princess Nicholas, by the renowned painter Philip de Laszlo.

Most magnificent of all were the jewels Princess Marina received. From Queen Mary there was an entire suite of sapphires and diamonds – tiara, necklace, brooches and earrings – a diamond and pearl sautoir from the King and Queen; a pearl and diamond scroll tiara as well as a large diamond bow brooch from Princess Nicholas; and, from the Duke of Kent himself, a ruby and diamond bracelet, and an antique necklace of 372 pearls with diamond motifs.

On the day before the wedding Bertie and Elizabeth, the Duke and Duchess of York, gave a luncheon party at their home, 145 Piccadilly, for George and Marina, and that night the couple were accompanied by Queen Mary when they attended a performance of *Theatre Royal* at the Lyric Theatre in Shaftesbury Avenue. *The Times* reported:

> The visit to the theatre took the audience completely by surprise. The royal party waited until the lights had been dimmed in preparation for the curtain to go up before taking their seats. As the Queen walked to the front of the box she was immediately recognized by the audience, who stood and applauded. When Princess Marina and the Duke of Kent appeared in the second box there was a great burst of cheering and clapping, which the Duke and the Princess acknowledged by waving . . . to the audience. The rising of the curtain was delayed by two minutes owing to the spontaneous welcome of the audience. In an interval Miss

Prince George with his grandmother (Princess Marina's great-aunt) Queen Alexandra.

(Right) Prince George (*centre*) with his younger brother Prince John (*left*) and their cousin, Prince Olav of Norway, circa 1910.

Princess Nicholas of Greece with her three daughters, Elizabeth (*left*), Marina (*standing*) and Olga.

(Right) George and Marina, Duke and Duchess of Kent, photographed at Himley Hall, Staffordshire, during the first part of their honeymoon.

The wedding of Prince George, Duke
of Kent and Princess Marina, 29
November 1934. The wedding group
in the Throne Room of Buckingham
Palace shows: (*front row, left to right*)
Olga, Princess Paul of Yugoslavia;
Queen Maud of Norway; Princess
Nicholas of Greece; King George v; the
bride and bridegroom; Queen Mary;
King Christian x of Denmark; Queen
Alexandrine of Denmark. (*Back row,
left to right*) Prince Paul of Yugoslavia
(*second left*); Prince Waldemar of
Denmark; Prince George of Greece;
Princess Victoria; King George II of
Greece; Prince Nicholas of Greece. The
youngest bridesmaids are Lady Mary
Cambridge (*left*) and Princess
Elizabeth of York (now Queen
Elizabeth II).

(Above left) The Duchess of Kent, President of Alexandra Rose, receiving a bouquet of 'Alexandra roses' outside her London home, 3 Belgrave Square, in June 1937.

(Above right) Noël Coward's photograph of Princess Marina with Alexandra in the garden of his home in 1937.

Cecil Beaton's portrait of Princess Marina, Duchess of Kent, 1938.

(Left) The Duke and Duchess of Kent arriving at the People's Palace in East London to attend a children's concert conducted by Malcolm Sargent, 1937.

(Left) Against a background influenced by Fragonard, Marina is photographed by Cecil Beaton wearing a Greek-style gown of sky-blue taffeta and a hat wreathed in flowers.

(Opposite left) George and Marina's greetings card to Noël Coward, Christmas 1940.

(Opposite right) The Duke and Duchess visiting a hospital for the old and infirm, London, 1940.

(Opposite below) Coppins in Iver, Buckinghamshire, left to Prince George by his aunt, Princess Victoria.

The Duchess wearing the suite of sapphires and diamonds given to her as a wedding present by Queen Mary.

Best wishes for Xmas, 1940.

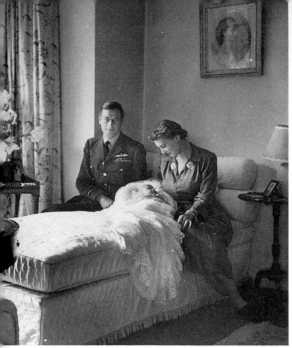

(Top left) The Duke and Duchess of Kent with the infant Prince Michael, photographed at Coppins on 15 August 1942.

(Top right) George, Duke of Kent, with his elder son Eddie, August 1942. Ten days after this photograph was taken, George was killed in a flying accident in Scotland.

(Bottom) Marina reading to Eddie and Alexandra.

George and Marina at home. Coppins, August 1942.

(Opposite above) An aerial view of the crash site which Andrew Jack, the sole survivor of the disaster, kept among his possessions. The wreckage of the Sunderland is seen as white fragments (*centre right and left*), while the scorched heather is clearly visible.

(Opposite below) The twisted propellors of the crashed Sunderland W4026.

(Above) The coffin of Prince George, Duke of Kent, arriving at London's Euston Station on its way to Windsor, 28 August 1942.

(Right) A wartime photograph of the Duchess as Commandant of the Women's Royal Naval Service (WRENS).

Marina and Eddie
during their tour of the
Far East in 1952.

Exchanging gifts with
the Sultan of Brunei;
the Duchess of Kent
receives a silver casket
and a bolt of dress
material, 1952.

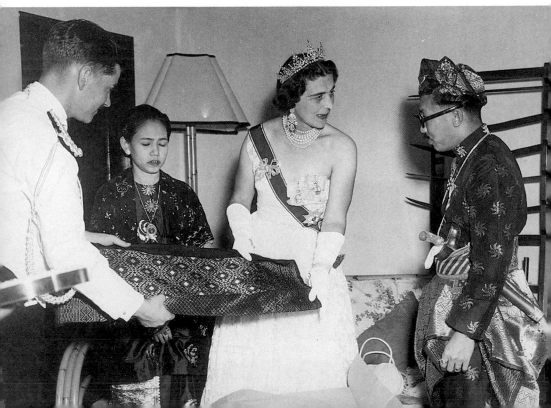

Noël Coward takes the Duchess of Kent's arm as they leave a London theatre with Princess Alexandra, after attending a charity midnight matinée during the late 1950s.

The Duchess presenting the 1956 Women's Championship trophy to the American tennis player Shirley Fry at Wimbledon. Her opponent, Angela Buxton, looks on.

(Above) The wedding of Edward, Duke of Kent, and Miss Katharine Worsley 8 June 1961. The group includes Princess Alexandra (*left*), Princess Marina, the Queen, Prince Michael of Kent, the bride and bridegroom, Sir William and Lady Worsley, Princess Anne, Prince Charles, Prince Philip and the Queen Mother.

(Opposite below) Princess Marina, the Earl and Countess of Airlie, Princess Anne and the Hon. Peregrine Fairfax (best man) join the bride and bridegroom in this group photograph taken at St James's Palace, after the wedding of Princess Alexandra and the Hon. Angus Ogilvy, 24 April 1963.

(Right) Princess Marina chatting to Princess Alice, Countess of Athlone, on the steps of St Paul's Cathedral, after a service commemorating the fiftieth anniversary of the Order of the British Empire, May 1967. Both Princesses were Dames Grand Cross of the Order.

(Below) The coffin of Princess Marina, Duchess of Kent, is borne from St George's Chapel, Windsor Castle, 30 August 1968.

The last formal portrait of Princess Marina, taken by Cecil Beaton at Kensington Palace during the summer of 1964.

Marie Tempest, Miss Madge Titheradge, and Mr Laurence Olivier were presented to the Queen.

The Duke of Kent and his fiancée were cheered by a great crowd when they left the theatre. As their car was driven away thousands surged forward through the police barrier, and women ran to the side of the car waving their handkerchiefs in greeting.

The Duke and the Princess were given a tumultuous ovation when the royal cars arrived at Piccadilly Circus. The large crowd swarmed round and cheered wildly. The escort of police cars and the police on duty had difficulty in clearing a way. The Queen was in the first car, and the Duke of Kent and Princess Marina could be seen smiling happily in the other. Instead of going down Piccadilly the cars turned up Regent Street and then proceeded via Bond Street, where the large crowds who were viewing the decorations cheered the royal party all the way.

Thursday 29 November was all the weather forecasters said it would be: a typically grey, damp, misty winter's day without so much as a hint of sunshine. The street lamps were still on at midday. Nevertheless, the crowds still thronged the royal route from Buckingham Palace to Westminster Abbey and back, people hung from every available window and rooftop the carriage processions would pass, and the vast red and blue stands in Parliament Square had started to fill with spectators well before dawn. The bells of the Abbey began ringing a full peal of more than 5,000 changes as soon as the first guests began arriving; the slippery roads were sanded; street vendors sold all manner of wedding souvenirs and favours; and the boys of Westminster School, traditional cheerleaders on occasions such as this, took up their specially appointed places near the Abbey's great West Door. Beneath the bare plane trees the bunting and flags, troops and military bands lining the streets were marshalled into position, while behind them plainclothes police kept a watch on the crowds.

At Buckingham Palace, in the white and gold Ball-Supper Room where the wedding breakfast was to be held, florists completed their arrangements of roses, carnations, chrysanthemums, heather and lilies of the valley, while the wedding cake was carefully set up on a table of its own. Topped with a trailing bouquet of roses, orange blossom and snowdrops, the four-tier confection – more a pseudo-Gothic work of art – stood nine feet tall and weighed 800 pounds. Made from 'Empire products, together with currants specially sent from Greece', each elaborately iced tier was decorated with bells, cupids, and the couple's entwined initials, while among the charms to be found inside were a wedding ring, a thimble, a threepenny bit, a horseshoe and a dove.

Amid all the pomp and splendour, there was one small incident concerning the bridegroom himself, which added a more mundane note to an occasion that had been rehearsed with clockwork precision. Just before he put on his ceremonial naval uniform, the Duke of Kent discovered that his wallet was almost empty. So, dressed in an everyday lounge suit, he slipped out of York House and walked unrecognized to his bank to cash a cheque.

'Surely you could have sent someone else', said an incredulous Prince of Wales, when his brother reappeared.

'Oh, easily,' George replied, 'but it gave me something to do.'

By 10.30 am the 2,000-strong congregation had taken their places at Westminster Abbey, in readiness for the arrival of the royal family. First came Mary, the Princess Royal, the Duchess of York and her four-year-old daughter Princess Margaret, dressed respectively in blue, pink and cream. With them were other royal guests including Prince and Princess Arthur of Connaught; Princess Alice, Countess of Athlone; and Lady Patricia Ramsay, the former Princess Patricia of Connaught who in 1919 had established the trend for royal weddings at Westminster Abbey. The bride's sisters – Princess Paul dressed in parchment satin, and Countess Toerring wearing china-blue velvet – were also among the first party of royal arrivals. Then came the King and Queen – he in the uniform of an Admiral of the Fleet, she in blue and gold – with Princess Nicholas of Greece in ivory and gold, Prince Waldemar of Denmark, the King and Queen of Norway, the King and Queen of Denmark, the King of Greece, and the Prince Regent of Yugoslavia.

The last to arrive before the bride herself, was, of course, the Duke of Kent, accompanied by the Prince of Wales and the Duke of York. Once the princes had taken their places at the foot of the Sacrarium steps, the scene was set for the entrance of Princess Marina and her father. Travelling in a closed semi-state landau attended by a Captain's Escort of the Life Guards, the bride had left Buckingham Palace at 10.46 am and, according to schedule, was expected to arrive at the Abbey's West Door twelve minutes later, at precisely 10.58. Before the high altar, on which was arrayed the Abbey's famous gold plate, waited the Archbishops of Canterbury and York, and the Bishop of London, together with the Metropolitan Germanos of Thyateira, Exarch of the Ecumenical Patriarchate in Western Europe, and the Great Archimandrite Michael Constantinidis. On the bridge of the organ screen with the choir waited the trumpeters who would sound a welcoming fanfare, while just inside the West Door stood Marina's eight bridesmaids. Dressed in white and silver and carrying bouquets of white roses, the six older attendants were the Princesses Eugenie, Irene and Katherine of Greece, Princess Juliana of the Netherlands, Princess Kyra of Russia, and Lady Iris Mountbatten. The two youngest bridesmaids, wearing short dresses of stiffened white tulle, so that the King could see 'their pretty little knees', were Princess Elizabeth of York and Lady Mary Cambridge.

Then, at last, to the cacophonous sounds of pealing bells, cheering crowds, and the bellowed orders of those commanding troops on ceremonial duty, the bride arrived. For her wedding, Princess Marina had chosen a shimmering gown of supple silver and white brocaded lamé, patterned with English roses. Its cowl neckline was softly draped and the long, trumpet sleeves finished in deep, turned-back cuffs faced with plain silver. From her shoulders fell a court train, twelve feet in length, and this too was lined in silver. Securing a full veil of white silk tulle, the Princess wore a diamond fringe tiara given to her by the City of London. To complete the picture, Marina wore diamond earrings, a matching necklace and a small bar brooch; while pinned to her left shoulder was the private order of the royal family, given to her by the King. That order consisted of an oval miniature of George v surrounded by diamonds, fastened by a diamond crown to a bow of pale blue watered silk. The bouquet Marina carried was of creamy-white madonna lilies, finished with a satin ribbon embossed with the Duke of Kent's coat of arms.

As the last notes of the trumpet flourish faded away, the organ and the choir burst into song and, to Sir John Stainer's hymn 'Gracious Spirit, Holy Ghost', Prince Nicholas led his youngest daughter along the nave towards her bridegroom. After the Dean of Westminster had opened the service, the Archbishop of Canterbury stepped forward to marry the Duke of Kent and Princess Marina:

'George Edward Alexander Edmund, wilt thou have this woman to thy wedded wife, to live together after God's ordinance in the holy estate of matrimony? Wilt thou love her, comfort her, honour and keep her, in sickness and in health; and, forsaking all other, keep thee only unto her, so long as ye both shall live?'

'I will,' responded the Duke.

The Archbishop then turned to the bride with the same charge: 'Marina, wilt thou have this man to thy wedded husband . . .?'

'I will,' the Princess replied softly but firmly.

'Who giveth this woman to be married to this man?' asked the Archbishop. Quietly Prince Nicholas gave Marina's hand to the Primate, and George and Marina then took their vows. At that point, the Prince of Wales, as best man, should have produced the ring to be blessed. But, when his mother glanced at him, David seemed to be miles away. Queen Mary touched her husband's arm, and unobtrusively the King signalled to his son. Immediately the Prince took the ring from his pocket. Placing it on the open prayer book, the Archbishop continued, 'In thy name, O Lord, we hallow and dedicate this ring, that by thy blessing he who gives it and she who wears it, keeping true faith the one to the other, may abide together in thy peace. . . .' Moments later, the Archbishop loudly proclaimed, 'Those whom God hath joined together let no man put asunder.'

At the end of the ceremony the new Duchess of Kent was led by her husband across the Sacrarium – where, four hunded years earlier, Elizabeth I had sometimes knelt in prayer – into the Chapel of St Edward the Confessor. There the marriage registers were signed and congratulations offered by the officiating clergy. With the Anglican service over, George and Marina, Duke and Duchess of Kent, retraced their steps back along the nave to the bridal march from *Lohengrin* – better known perhaps as 'Here Comes the Bride' – followed by Mendelssohn's Wedding March.

Beyond the West Door, the Abbey bells pealed yet again and the crowd roared its greeting to the Duke and Duchess. Once the pair were settled in their carriage, this time the Glass Coach, the drive back to Buckingham Palace began. *En route* the bride and bridegroom slowly passed St George's Hospital at Hyde Park Corner, where nursing staff and some of the patients waited to see them. This was an important moment for the Duke of Kent, not only because he was president of the hospital, but because, at his request, the nation's wedding present to Marina and himself took the form of a large donation to the hospital's rebuilding fund.

As soon as they had returned to Buckingham Palace the Duke and Duchess, together with their families, made their way to the private chapel (nowadays the Queen's Gallery) for the Greek Orthodox ceremony. That service, which lasted for half an hour, combined the rites for betrothal and for marriage, the principal feature of the former being the exchange of wedding rings; and of the latter the joining of the bridal couple's hands, their crowning – with jewelled crowns specially made for the occasion – which was symbolic of blessing, their drinking from a common cup of wine in token 'of their sharing one lot for weal or woe', and the procession thrice around the nuptial table, representing their journey through life together. Apart from the final blessing, which was delivered in English, the rest of the service was conducted by the Metropolitan and the Great Archimandrite entirely in Greek.

After the observance of all the religious formalities, the family photographs, and the obligatory balcony appearances, the bride and bridegroom, their parents and guests could finally relax at the wedding breakfast. On the menu were *Filet de sole*, *Côtes d'agneau braisées*, *Perdreaux à la crême*, *Pêches Melba* and *Corbeilles de friandises*. Two hours later, after the Duke and Duchess had cut their wedding cake using the bridegroom's ceremonial sword, it was time for the couple to change into their going-away outfits; the Duke into a dark lounge suit and overcoat, the Duchess into a dress and jacket of almond green wool trimmed with nutria fur, an ankle-length sable coat and a pale green velvet turban.

Shortly after four o'clock George and Marina climbed into an open landau and, chased by members of their families throwing rose petals and tiny silver horseshoes, drove off through Hyde Park towards Paddington Station. It was the start of a five-month honeymoon that would begin at Himley Hall, the Earl of Dudley's estate in Staffordshire; continue at Trent Park, the home of Sir Philip Sassoon, near Barnet; and end, after Christmas at Sandringham, with a cruise in the West Indies. Of their arrival at Paddington that afternoon, *The Times* told its readers:

There were the usual false alarms and cheers, but the arrival of the Duke and Duchess was unmistakable enough; in the distance a faint cheering which moved slowly steadily nearer, gathering in volume all the while like the approach of a distant hurricane. The cheering outran the royal carriage. Long before it was in sight the crowd was shouting welcome, and even then the open carriage with the smiling Duke and Duchess had disappeared beneath the long glass roof before the welcome could be changed to *au revoir*. Then came the King and Queen in their closed car, to an even mightier cheer.

George v and Queen Mary had, unusually, followed the honeymoon couple to bid them yet another farewell and to spend a few more minutes with them in the privacy of the station's royal reception room. Then the Duke and Duchess stepped through crimson and gold drapes, decorated with a horseshoe of white chrysanthemums, onto the brightly lit platform, covered with deep red carpeting, banks of flowers and special stands full of applauding spectators. At 4.35 pm the royal train pulled out of the station and Marina and her husband settled back in their wood-panelled compartment full of yellow roses and bronze chrysanthemums, for the 110-mile journey to Birmingham's Snow Hill station. As the train sped through five counties on its way up to the Midlands that night, groups of people turned out to watch it pass. At High Wycombe the train slowed to acknowledge a crowd of about 1,000 people; near Aynho Junction, wellwishers set off fireworks in greeting, while at Leamington, where an estimated 3,000 people waited in the hope of catching a glimpse of the Duke and Duchess, men at the ironworks released a vast plume of blue and crimson flame into the black sky.

At Snow Hill, where the train arrived ten minutes late, George and Marina were welcomed by the Lord Mayor of Birmingham, whose wife presented the Duchess with a bouquet of roses, tied with ribbons in the Greek national colours of blue and white. After greeting members of the official reception committee, the Duke and his bride were led out to their waiting car and driven through the city's crowded streets towards Dudley and Himley Hall itself.

Among the messages of congratulations George v received from around the world, the most ironic must surely have been that from President Zaimis of Greece. His message read: 'On the occasion of the happy marriage of the Duke of Kent with Princess Marina, I ask you to accept my congratulations and wishes for the happiness of the bridal pair and of the members of the royal family and the prosperity of the great British nation.' It was, no doubt, a sincere enough gesture, but the truer feelings of the Greeks themselves were more accurately reflected in a letter which the American diplomat Lincoln McVeagh wrote to President Roosevelt from Athens on 4 December:

> You will have seen a lot in the American papers about the marriage of Princess Marina of Greece to the Duke of Kent. There is some sentiment, or sentimentality, about that here too. But almost fifty per cent of the population of Greece would emphasize to any inquirer that the Princess has no Greek blood and no Greek passport. . . . Royalist propaganda is noticeably absent.

In less than a year, popular sentiment in Athens would tell a very different story. George II of Greece would be restored to his throne once again, the Greek royal family would be back in their villas and palaces, and 'royalist propaganda' would be anything but absent.

Chapter Nine

Private Lives

It was, coincidentally, while they were on honeymoon in the Caribbean in March 1935 that George and Marina first met America's thirty-second President in person. Then in his second year in office, Franklin D. Roosevelt was visiting Nassau aboard Vincent Astor's yacht *Nourmahal*. Perhaps because his curiosity had been aroused by Lincoln McVeagh's recent letter, or simply because they happened to be in the same place at the same time, the President invited the Duke and Duchess to lunch with him.

To many Americans, who still seemed to think that England and the English had not progressed much beyond gas lighting and horse-drawn carriages, the general concept of royalty was no more advanced – though, to be fair, when the British monarchy was represented by remote and reactionary figureheads like King George v and Queen Mary, much could be forgiven. Nevertheless, if President Roosevelt had expected George and Marina to be courteous and attentive, but otherwise vapid and out of touch, he was to be pleasantly surprised. In them he found spontaneity coupled with intellect and an unaffected charm; qualities which he, not unnaturally, considered highly attractive. Equally, if little more than diplomacy on their part had led the Duke and Duchess to lunch with the former Governor of New York, they, too, were to be captivated. Almost from the moment they met on 27 March a cordial friendship was established; so much so that when they parted later that afternoon, there was no doubting the sincerity of the President's invitation to 'come and see me in Washington'. So taken were the Duke and Duchess for their part that that same evening Prince George cabled Roosevelt aboard the *Nourmahal*, 'My wife and I will always retain the happiest memories of our delightful, informal, meeting today. We both wish you health, happiness and a successful administration and look forward to seeing you again in the near future.'

The Kents' protracted honeymoon finally came to an end on 14 April. When they returned to London that day they drove straight to their new home, Number 3 Belgrave Square, a few minutes' walk from Hyde Park in one direction and the garden of Buckingham Palace in the other. All the houses in Belgrave Square, like many others in the vicinity, were tall, uniformly white and elegant; the legacy of Thomas Cubitt, famous nineteenth-century builder and architect.

Number 3 was owned by Lady Juliet Duff, daughter of the celebrated Lady Ripon, and it was she who leased the house to the Duke and Duchess with the generous provision that they could redecorate and refurnish as they wished. For George, with his instinctive flair for interior decoration, the temptation to make changes was irresistible. 'His sense of decorative values', as James Wentworth-Day wrote, 'was so sure that he could order silks, brocades, chintzes and colours with the eye and appreciation of a woman.' Even Marina had to admit that she left everything to her husband's judgement. The Dowager Lady Airlie recalled:

> In the 1930s I often dined at the Duke and Duchess of Kent's house in Belgrave Square, and I was always impressed not so much by the externals of happiness – the brilliance of the conversation, the beautifully arranged rooms and the perfectly chosen meal – as by the deeper harmony of two temperaments.
>
> Once when I complimented the Duchess on the dinner she laughed. 'I am really a very bad hostess. I must confess that I didn't know what we were going to eat tonight until the food appeared. My husband chose the dinner and the wine – and the flowers and everything else. He enjoys doing it, and so I always leave the household affairs to him. I let him make all the decisions over furniture and decorations. He has a wonderful sense of colour and design.

For a woman like Marina, who was far from submissive by nature, taking a back seat in this way was a very considerable compliment to the talents of her husband. Before long George had devised new colour schemes for most of the rooms, using a wide range of skilfully blended pastel shades, both to enhance the antique and contemporary furnishings and to act as a subtle backdrop to his collection of pictures and *objets d'art*. The house was not without its more dramatic touches, however, and it has been said that Marina's own bathroom was decorated in black and silver; though, if true, this was but a derivation of Juliet Duff's original theme of black and gold.

Marina herself was not without taste or ideas in home decoration and, by casually remarking that she would not like her house 'to look like a bar', unwittingly damped the trend for chrome furniture and what were described as 'razzle-dazzle' cushions and curtains. The sayings, doings, likes and dislikes of royalty have always influenced public thinking, at least among those to whom such things matter. And in exactly the same way that Diana, Princess of Wales, has been acknowledged as a leader of fashion both at home and abroad, so Marina also had an enormous influence in her day. Colours, such as 'Marina blue', were named in her honour; women took up smoking, simply because it was known the Duchess of Kent smoked; her hairstyles were copied; and some even tried to emulate the way in which she walked. Yet Marina's greatest influence by far was on the style of women's clothing. She started a craze for small pillbox hats and turbans – with or without the adornment of feather trims and light net veils – and also, like the present Princess Royal during the early 1970s, created a vogue for wide-brimmed hats, even though it was a rule that royal women were never to wear anything that might hide or obscure their faces. She helped to make trousers acceptable among 'respectable' women, and did everything to revive interest in cotton. 'When she first came to England', said one textile manufacturer at the time, 'no really smart woman would have worn a cotton dress, but the Duke told her of the depression in Lancashire and the desperate poverty of many of the people. She asked her dressmaker to design cotton frocks for her and wore them ... until the fashion was firmly established.'

Marina's interest in clothes and her own ability as a needle-woman had first surfaced many years earlier in Paris, when she would design and run up dresses for herself. According to Jennifer Ellis, writing in the early 1950s, the Duchess had three secrets for successful dressing:

She never lets herself be influenced by the fact that something
is the latest style, if she does not think it would suit her.
She never minds being seen in the same dress several times.
And she always chooses clothes that are interchangeable.
In her wardrobe no hat goes with just one pair of shoes and
no other, and most of her scarves and stoles have reversible
linings.

Later on, during the Second World War, when clothing coupons
ruled out even the smallest extravagance, Marina's resourceful-
ness and versatility are said to have led her to make several summer dresses 'from material which had been bought before the
war for curtains'.

One of the most glowing tributes to Marina's sense of style
was made by the couturier John Cavanagh, who not only created
many of her most successful outfits, but was to design the wedding
dresses of the present Duchess of Kent in 1961, and Princess Alexandra in 1963. Now retired, he began his career at the House
of Molyneux in Paris. Mr Cavanagh told the author,

I worshipped Princess Marina from the very first moment
I set eyes on her. To me she was sheer magic and always
remained my dream woman, personifying superb elegance.
Later she was often my inspiration. She was, from the word
go, the woman I wanted to dress more than any other in
the world. I never dreamt in those early days that I would
one day have that great honour and immense pleasure.

While elegance and style were inherent in Princess Marina as in
no other female member of the royal family, one aspect of her
'look' did not receive royal approval. Quite early on Queen Mary
made it known that George v disliked her painting her fingernails.
'Your George might not like it,' retorted Marina, 'but mine does!'
The subject was never mentioned again.

It was at 3 Belgrave Square on 9 October 1935 that the Duchess
of Kent gave birth to the first of her three children. By the time
she and George returned from their honeymoon Marina was
already three months pregnant and, when it came to redecorating
their new home, the Duke, perhaps anticipating the birth of a
son, chose a blue and white colour scheme for the top-floor
nursery.

At the beginning of October, Marina's parents came to London for the birth of their first Kent grandchild, whose arrival was then expected on the sixteenth. Among Prince and Princess Nicholas's first visitors was Chips Channon, George and Marina's neighbour in Belgrave Square. He noted in his diary on 7 October:

> I went to Claridge's to have tea with the Nicholases of Greece. The Duchess of Kent was there in a brown dress and much bejewelled, and rather large. . . . She was sweetness itself, but she has not become in the least English . . . . At one point the Grand Duchess [Princess Nicholas] sent her daughter into the next room to fetch her spectacles and the Duchess went meekly. She has been well brought up in an old-fashioned, affectionate way.

Channon, who also had a keen eye for the men and found the Duke of Kent 'altogether irresistible', followed Marina's pregnancy with great interest, partly out of friendship and partly because his own wife, the former Lady Honor Guinness, was expecting their first, and only, child at much the same time. In the event, and to Channon's wild delight, both women gave birth on the very same day.

On the evening of 8 October, when it became clear that the Duchess's baby would be born at any hour, Fleet Street sent newsmen hotfoot to 3 Belgrave Square, where they assembled in a ground-floor room. Shortly before midnight the Duke of Kent put his head round the door. 'I just thought I'd tell you that some hot coffee is being sent in to you,' he said. 'After that I'm afraid the kitchens will be closed, but there'll be someone on duty just after six who will get you some breakfast.' Then he added, 'I do hope it'll be over soon. I don't think I could stand much more of this.'

The journalists did not have to wait for breakfast. At 2.15 am Princess Marina gave birth to a son. Edward George Nicholas Paul Patrick, as the child was christened at Buckingham Palace on 20 November, was King George and Queen Mary's fifth grandchild and, to add to their pleasure, he was born in what was an especially memorable year for the royal family.

At St Paul's Cathedral on 6 May the nation had celebrated the silver jubilee of George v's reign. It was, of course, an occasion of the greatest pomp and circumstance, and one on which Marina was singled out yet again for her elegant appearance, even though she was wearing one of her frowned-upon wide-brimmed hats, this time a vast creamy-fawn platter trimmed with ostrich feathers. Later that year, only four weeks after the birth of Prince Edward of Kent, or 'Eddie' as he was called, yet another royal occasion caught the public's imagination. This time it was the wedding, in the chapel at Buckingham Palace on 6 November, of Prince Henry, Duke of Gloucester, and Lady Alice Montagu-Douglas-Scott, daughter of the seventh Duke of Buccleuch. Within the space of six months the King had celebrated his silver jubilee, the birth of his third grandson, and the marriage of his third son. But the happiness each of those events had given him, was suddenly marred by the death, on 3 December, of his favourite sister Princess Victoria.

Born on 6 July 1868, 'Toria' was the second of Edward vii's three daughters and the only one of them never to have married. That she was to die a meddlesome and embittered spinster was due entirely to the fact that her mother, Queen Alexandra, kept her at home to act as her companion and nursemaid. Yet Toria, whose heart ached for romance, was not without her suitors. One member of the Baring family, for instance, would gladly have married her, as indeed would the considerably older, and widowed, prime minister Lord Rosebery. Another of her admirers, though also old enough to be her father, was Admiral Fisher. He was to write of her in early middle age, 'Princess Victoria, who used to be scraggy, lanky and anaemic, has developed into an opulent figure with a rosy, plump face! She looked very handsome and I told her so, and her tall figure makes her most imposing now.'

As a result of her mother's selfishness Princess Victoria grew old before her time, becoming vaguely eccentric and seeking solace in illness, both real and imagined. When Queen Alexandra died in 1925 Toria was already fifty-seven and, in a sense, homeless. From childhood she had lived with her parents, first at Marlborough House in London – where she was born – and at Sandringham in Norfolk. With her father's accession to the throne in 1901 Toria moved to Buckingham Palace, but nine years later, when Edward vii died, she and her mother were obliged to return to Marlborough House. Thus the Princess spent most of her life shuffling monotonously between London and East Anglia. When she was at last free of her demanding mother Toria looked for a home of her own, and found what she was searching for in a rambling farmhouse near the village of Iver in Buckinghamshire. Originally known as The Coppins – the prefix was dropped some years later – Princess Victoria had the house rebuilt, furnished it in the heavy style of the Victorians and, apart from her servants, lived there on her own.

Lending structure, if not purpose, to the Princess's sad and rather meaningless existence were the closeness of her relationship with her brother George v and the interest she took in village life. A familiar figure in Iver, where she played the part of Lady Bountiful to perfection, the Princess would often visit the local school, but rarely if ever went in. Instead, she would stand in the playground peering through the classroom windows, waving and calling to the children.

Fond of whisky, Toria was never without a plentiful supply, which was good news for Parker her chauffeur, who was equally partial to his employer's favourite tipple. Like so many who take an illicit drink when on duty, Parker was never without a bag of strong mints in his uniform pocket. The ruse apparently worked for a time until one day, from the back of the car, the Princess exclaimed, 'Parker, I don't mind you going into my room to have a nip of my whisky, but I wish you wouldn't suck those dreadful mints to disguise the fact that you do it.'

Almost every day Princess Victoria and her brother spoke on the telephone, and there is a well-known story which, apart from being amusing, provides an insight into the kind of relationship she and the gruff old King – whose abrupt manner frightened his more timid relations – always shared. Having put through a call to him, the Princess heard a click and shouted down the line, 'Is that you, you old bugger?' Taken aback, the palace telephonist replied, 'I'm sorry, your Royal Highness, His Majesty is not yet on the line.'

The death of Princess Victoria at the age of sixty-seven is generally believed to have hastened the end of the King's life. In failing health for some years, George v cancelled the State Opening of Parliament and shortly after Toria's funeral at Frogmore, a mile or so from Windsor Castle through the private Home Park, he retired to Sandringham. That December, the King made what was to be his last Christmas broadcast to the Empire, planted a cedar tree in front of Sandringham House, rode his 'fat little shooting pony' around the estate and, as he wrote in his diary, 'saw my Kent grandson in his bath'. On 12 January 1936 the King, breathless, lethargic and feeling generally unwell, took to his bed. He died eight days later at 11.55 pm on Monday 20 January.

The remains of George v were borne from Sandringham to London on 23 January, and for five days lay in state at Westminster Hall. It was there, at midnight on the twenty-seventh, that the Duke of Kent and his three elder brothers – the new King Edward viii, the Duke of York and the Duke of Gloucester – paid a unique tribute to their father. Dressed in ceremonial uniform and with swords reversed and heads bowed, they joined officers of the Household Brigade, who took up one of the twenty-minute watches observed at the foot of the catafalque. Queen Mary was so moved by her sons' gesture that she commissioned F. E. Beresford to commemorate the scene in a painting entitled *The Vigil of the Princes*. On the following day, 28 January, in a long and solemn pageant, the King's coffin was removed to Windsor, where it was interred in St George's Chapel.

Chapter Ten

Year of the Three Kings

In much the same way that the royal family never answer questions about personal wealth, so the contents of royal wills are never disclosed. Though certain bequests of specific public interest are occasionally made known, details concerning the more sensitive areas of who inherited what and how much always remain jealously guarded secrets. To what extent, therefore, the Duke of Kent benefited from the Will of George v is an unanswerable question. One bequest to the Kents that was made public, however, emanated from the Will of George's late aunt Toria. On New Year's Day 1936 it was announced that she had left Coppins, her private estate, to the young Duke and his family.

Today Iver in Buckinghamshire is no longer the picturesque, rural village that George and Marina – and indeed Princess Victoria – once knew. There are, admittedly, traces of what used to be, particularly in the immediate vicinity of the Church of St Peter, where the Kents used to worship and where George would take his Alsatian dog Doushka for a casual stroll. But otherwise much of Iver's charm has been obliterated by subsequent development; an incongruous parade of glass-fronted shops, for example, and concrete roundabouts at road junctions.

Coppins itself lies in a largely unspoilt area of countryside on Bangors Road South, about a mile outside the village. The house, set in extensive grounds which once included Princess Victoria's model farm, is approached through wrought-iron gates at the top of a curving drive. Originally built in 1850, Coppins can claim no great architectural merit, but even today, almost twenty years after the present Duke of Kent sold it, the two-storey house with its many-gabled roofs sprouting numerous chimneys, its black-painted shutters and white walls looks exactly the same as it did when George and Marina lived there.

Between March and June 1936 considerable alterations were made to the house before the Duke and Duchess adopted it as their country home. A curiously angled porch was demolished together with a verandah which Princess Victoria had built so that she and her guests might enjoy the view of the lawns and the countryside beyond; most of the original fireplaces were taken out in favour of modern replacements, while George, the keenest motorist in the royal family, had the existing garage pulled down and a new one, featuring high-pressure hoses and air supply, built to his own specifications. Inside the house, once Princess Victoria's possessions had been removed the Duke of Kent dispelled the Victorian gloom by again using delicate colour schemes, light pine panelling and bright furnishing fabrics. (One of the few items belonging to Princess Victoria that the Kents did keep, incidentally, was a marble bust of Edward VII, which was allowed to remain in the entrance hall.) To let in more light, he tackled the garden's heavy vegetation and helped fell trees that restricted daylight.

While the builders and decorators were at work George and Marina paid frequent visits to Coppins and, on one particular Friday in April, they were accompanied by Queen Mary, the Duke and Duchess of York, Princess Alice and Lord Athlone, with whom they had been lunching at Royal Lodge, the Yorks' pink-stuccoed mansion in Windsor Great Park.

Of the rooms on the ground floor – which also included a dining room to seat fourteen, and two sitting rooms – the large music room with its tall glass doors opening on to the garden became the main salon. Here, George would listen to jazz records, play his Ibeck baby grand or the larger Steinway, or quietly sit and read while Marina painted at her easel, set up on a dustsheet spread over the carpet. Here also the Kents would entertain their friends. On any evening Noël Coward might be found at Coppins, as might Malcolm Sargent, Somerset Maugham, Douglas Fairbanks and an assortment of relations including George's cousin Dickie Mountbatten and his wife Edwina. Other welcome guests were the Channons, who first visited towards the end of 1936. Chips Channon wrote in his diary on 1 November:

We drove down to Coppins to call on the Kents. They have modernised and re-decorated it with skill and success. The result is charming, and the rooms now glow with luxe and gaiety. It is entirely Prince George who has transformed it, and he now thinks of little else. We had a massive tea, and then the besotted father carried in . . . the curly-haired, very red Prince Edward [who] looks like all four [Hanoverian] Georges rolled into one.

There were also occasions that year when the King and Mrs Simpson drove over from Sunningdale either for tea or for cocktails; and in return George and Marina were often entertained at the Fort. Whether it was because they were generally more open-minded than the rest of the royal family, or were simply less willing to condemn people out of hand, Prince George and Princess Marina rather liked Wallis Simpson. It is true, of course, that their feelings cooled after the Abdication – at one point, George became so angry and distressed that he said he wanted to kill Mrs Simpson – but when the crisis passed and tempers subsided, the relationship was restored.

It is also true that in 1937 the Duchess of Kent flatly refused to visit the Duke and Duchess of Windsor, as Edward and Wallis had by then become, when she and her husband were on holiday in the Tyrol. Since nothing would move Marina, George made the trip to Castle Wasserleonburg in Carinthia on his own. When he arrived he found his wife's snub repaid in kind and, while George saw his brother, Wallis made sure he did not see her. In time the hurt of that episode also passed and, with affections rekindled, Princess Marina – as her daughter Alexandra confirms – never lost touch with the Duke and Duchess of Windsor again.

British history books record 1936 as 'The Year of the Three Kings'. On 1 January the reign of George v had only twenty days left to run. By 31 December the reign of his second son and namesake George vi was exactly twenty days old. Between had fallen the historic eleven-month reign of King Edward viii.

Court mourning for George v meant that for the first few months of the year the Duke and Duchess of Kent were virtually free of public engagements. Privately they had more than enough to do and for the Duke, as we have seen, the refurbishment of Coppins was high on the list of priorities. For the Duchess official inactivity that spring meant that she could slip in extra visits to her own family. Ever since their childhood Marina and her sisters had shared an affinity that was unusual in a family of women. Throughout their lives, despite the inevitable responsibilities of adulthood, marriage and family life, they were ever in constant touch, exchanging long letters, long telephone calls and long visits. Not surprisingly, issues of motherhood had taken their allotted place in the sisters' thoughts and conversations, from the time Princess Olga's sons Alexander and Nicholas were born. Now with Woolly the mother of Hans Viet, her first child born in January 1935, and Marina the devoted mother of Prince Eddie, nine months younger than his German cousin, the three women had even more to talk about.

It was with children in mind that George and Marina set out for Belgrade at the beginning of April. For the past month Prince and Princess Paul had been settling into their newly built home, an impressive Regency-style mansion approached through an avenue of lime trees, and which Paul had called Beli Dvor. It was there on 7 April that Olga gave birth to her third and final child, a longed-for daughter, whom they named Jelisavetta (Elisabeth), and to whom George and Marina were to act as godparents.

Though it was far too early for anyone to be certain at that stage, Marina was again pregnant; and confirmation of that fact led to a small family celebration when she and George paid yet another holiday visit to Belgrade in June. Two months later Prince Paul, both as Regent and as a personal friend, received Marina's brother-in-law King Edward VIII when he paid a fleeting visit to Yugoslavia. The brevity of the King's stay that August suited Paul very well, since David had Mrs Simpson in tow and neither he nor Olga approved of the relationship that would soon cause a sensation throughout the world and bring scandal to the British monarchy. As a result of Prince Paul's attitude the atmosphere during the royal visit was at best strained. The Duchess of Windsor recalled in her memoirs:

> The meeting between the Balkan Prince and the British monarch was hardly calculated to hearten either Foreign Office. In a Slavic style worthy of his mountain-chieftain forebears, Paul led us in a wild motorcade through the countryside, scattering peasants and chickens in a flurry of

blouses and feathers, curses and cackles. David had a number of comments on the excursion, the one that really amused me was 'This is just about what I expected. The only thing that bothers me is that I can't figure which he cares less about, the peasants or the chickens or us.'

Edward VIII's courtesy call on the Regent of Yugoslavia preceded the now famous cruise along the Dalmatian coast which he, Mrs Simpson, and a handful of friends took aboard Lady Yule's steam yacht the *Nahlin*. Planned as a purely private holiday, the voyage soon assumed all the trappings of an official royal progress. Everywhere they stopped, from Yugoslavia to Turkey, kings, presidents and prime ministers turned out in force to welcome the British sovereign and his party.

At home, the King's holiday was scarcely referred to by the press. Now and then a paragraph or two might appear, but even then no mention was ever made of David's companion. Not until 3 December, when the press could maintain its silence no longer, did the people of Britain and the Empire learn what had been headline news and common gossip throughout Europe and America for the past two or three months: the King was in love with, and intended to marry, the by now twice-divorced Wallis Simpson.

Everywhere alarm bells started to ring. Queen Mary, who branded Wallis an 'adventuress', was never more confirmed in her opinion that 'one divorce could seldom or never be justified, and to divorce twice, on any grounds whatsoever, was ... unthinkable'.

As heir presumptive, the Duke of York became near hysterical at the thought of what he might have to take upon himself, while the Duchess of York, ever Mrs Simpson's most bitter opponent, joined the chorus of 'Establishment' figures determined to vilify Wallis as some kind of unspeakable sorceress, bent on luring Edward VIII to his doom. Of the King's family, only the Duke of Kent wondered how David, as head of a Church that forbade divorce, could actually marry a divorcee *and* retain his throne. How, in one of the King's favourite expressions, did David think he would be able 'to get away with it'? And what of Wallis? What would she become? What, as the Duke of Kent asked his brother, would 'she call herself?'

'Call herself?' replied the King. 'What do you think? "Queen of England", of course!'

'She's going to be *Queen*?' George asked in amazement.

'Yes', cried the King, 'and Empress of India – the whole bag of tricks.'

In fact, making Wallis Queen was never laid down as a precondition of David's marriage. To begin with the King naturally wanted her to share his throne as Queen Consort, but when it became obvious, even to him, that that could never be, he reluctantly agreed to put forward the idea of a morganatic marriage, suggested to Wallis over lunch at Claridge's by Esmond Harmsworth, son of Lord Rothermere, Chairman of the Newspaper Proprietors' Association. In that eventuality, since the sovereign is also Duke of Lancaster, reasoned Harmsworth, an apt title for Wallis might be Duchess of Lancaster. In the event, the morganatic proposal got nowhere. The Dominion governments would never countenance it, any more than the British. At every turn the King was rebuffed. The choice was clear; he would have to renounce either Wallis or the crown.

On 16 November the King saw the Prime Minister, Stanley Baldwin, at Buckingham Palace. 'I understand that you and several members of the Cabinet have some fear of a constitutional crisis developing over my friendship with Mrs Simpson,' he said.

The Prime Minister replied that that was so, and advised the King that a marriage with 'a divorced woman with two husbands still living' would not receive 'the approbation of the country'. 'I pointed out to him', Baldwin said, 'that the position of the King's wife was different from the position of any other citizen in the country; it was part of the price which the King had to pay. His wife becomes Queen; the Queen becomes the Queen of the country; and therefore, in the choice of a Queen, the voice of the people must be heard.'

In reply the King told his premier that his marriage 'had become an indispensable condition to his continued existence', and added, 'I want you to be the first to know that I have made up my mind and nothing will alter it .... I mean to abdicate to marry Mrs Simpson.'

Baldwin was stunned, the royal family outraged and bitter, while the nation became as divided in its opinions as it remains to this day. Of course the King and Mrs Simpson became the only topic of conversation the length and breadth of the country, and on 25 November, Chips Channon confided to his diary:

> The possibility of a royal marriage is still the talk of London
> . . . . The Duke of Kent asked Kitty Brownlow [wife of the
> King's Lord-in-Waiting, Perry Brownlow] what she thought
> of 'this marriage'. Kitty tried to nance out, but he insisted.
> 'After all they are my relations.' Then he made an
> astonishing rejoinder: 'I am very discreet.' 'As discreet as
> a Chubb safe when you've given away all the keys,' Kitty
> retorted.

Almost a fortnight later, and only two days before the crisis reached its inexorable climax, Channon and his wife were at a dinner party given by Lady Cunard, when Chips was summoned to the telephone. Afterwards he wrote:

> I . . . recognised the Duchess of Kent's voice. She asked us
> to go and see her, and Honor and I stole away to 3 Belgrave
> Square . . . . For two days now the Duke of Kent has been
> with his brother at the Fort, never leaving him for a second
> and trying by every means in his power to persuade him
> to stay. The King told him that over two years ago while
> he knew that he was an excellent Prince of Wales and liked
> his job, he nevertheless felt that he could never 'stick' being
> King as he puts it, he was afraid of being a bad one. He
> could never tolerate the restrictions, the etiquette, the
> loneliness; so perhaps if this issue had not arisen, something
> else would have.

For weeks the people of the Empire, from colonial 'top brass' to the humblest of workers, had hung on to every word from London, denouncing or defending the King, depending on where their sympathies lay. In a prophetic letter written in early December to Lord Brabourne, governor of Bombay, R. A. ('Rab') Butler, who was then Under-Secretary of State at the India Office, said,

> I never give people my private views, but here they are. [The
> King] is a congenitally weak man with great personal charm,
> publicity sense, and some cunning . . . . He will abdicate and
> will be succeeded by a dull dog who will hold the declining

influence of the Church and whose fortunes will be linked with that of the middle class.

In less than a fortnight Rab's forecast had become a reality. Thursday 10 December threatened to be as dismal as the rest of that week, with fog hanging over the Thames Valley like a heavy, dank canopy. On Edward VIII's writing table in the magnificent octagonal drawing room at Fort Belvedere six copies of a document, embossed with the royal coat of arms and headed 'Instrument of Abdication', lay near a red leather despatch box, its lid bearing the words 'The King' in gold letters. At about 10 am the Dukes of York, Gloucester and Kent arrived and went immediately into the drawing room, where their elder brother awaited them. Moments later David sat down at the table and, for the last time in his brief reign, signed each of the papers 'Edward R.I.' 'It was all quite informal,' he recalled in his memoirs. 'When I had signed the last document I yielded the chair to my brothers, who in turn appended their signatures in their order of precedence.' Having discharged his last duty as King, David stepped outside: '. . . as if in harmony with the lifting of the almost intolerable pressure of the last few weeks', he wrote, 'the fog . . . had also lifted.'

The following afternoon, while lunching at the Fort with Winston Churchill, Edward VIII ceased to reign. When it was time for the future prime minister to take leave of his old friend, David walked with him down the short stretch of hall to the front door. The ex-King was to write:

> Something must have stirred in his mind. Tapping out the solemn measure with his walking-stick, he began to recite, as if to himself: 'He nothing common did or mean, Upon that memorable scene.' His resonant voice seemed to give an especial poignancy to these lines from the ode by Andrew Marvell, on the beheading of Charles I.

By morning David would be sailing towards France and a gratuitous exile that would end only with his death thirty-six years later, in May 1972. But before his midnight departure for Portsmouth, where he boarded the destroyer HMS *Fury*, there was his public farewell to the nation, which he broadcast from a room in the Augusta Tower at Windsor Castle. There were also his private farewells to his family. In the salon at Royal Lodge, where they had assembled after dinner to listen to David's speech on the radio, were Queen Mary, her sons Bertie, Harry and George; her daughter Mary, the Princess Royal; her brother 'Alge', the Earl of Athlone, and his wife Princess Alice. When he returned from the Castle, David – or 'Prince Edward', as Sir John Reith, Director-General of the BBC, had announced him – kissed his mother and each of his relations in turn and then, bowing to Bertie, now King George VI, said, 'God bless you, Sir! I hope you will be happier than your predecessor.'

That scene, so heavily charged with pathos, proved too much for the sobbing Duke of Kent. In anguish, he suddenly cried out, 'It isn't possible! It isn't happening!' George's distress at his brother's departure was undoubtedly far keener than that of any other member of his family. Because of the bond he and David, now Duke of Windsor, had shared for almost twenty years, George's misery stemmed from a genuine sense of personal loss. To others, such as the new King, his wife and mother, such sorrow as they may also have felt was outweighed by anger at what they considered to be David's dereliction of duty.

In her unpublished memoirs Lady Iris Mountbatten, the only child of 'Drino', Marquess of Carisbrooke and a grandson of Queen Victoria, recalled that Queen Mary 'actually seemed unchanged by the great loss of her eldest son. I could see no outward sign that she had been tormented by heartbreak . . . . It brought home to me a sense that I had always had, that my family was not motivated by love or human emotions.'

Whatever the feelings of David's relations that December, the familiar routine was quickly re-established and, as Christmas approached, most members of the royal family gathered as usual at Sandringham. Two notable absentees, however, were the Duke and Duchess of Kent. With the birth of their second child due at any time, they had decided to remain at 3 Belgrave Square, with Prince and Princess Nicholas as their guests. There on Christmas morning itself, while a lone street musician played carols nearby, Marina presented her husband with a daughter – Alexandra Helen Elizabeth Olga Christabel. The official announcement issued that afternoon and signed by the doctors, W. Gilliatt, A. E. Gow, and H. A. Richards, read: 'H. R. H. The Duchess of Kent was safely delivered of a daughter at 11.20 this morning. Her Royal Highness and the infant Princess are doing excellently.'

To celebrate the birth in traditional style, a battery of Royal Horse Artillery set up its guns in Hyde Park, at noon on Boxing Day, to fire a salute. This forty-one gun salute was echoed by another fired simultaneously from the Tower of London. Five days later still in celebratory mood, the baby's father seized new Year's Eve as an opportunity to dress up in a silver Tyrolean costume and to accompany Lady Caroline Paget and the Honourable David Herbert to the Chelsea Arts Ball.

In Austria, where George's outfit might have looked more at home, the Duke of Windsor had spent Christmas Day as the guest of Sir Walford and Lady Selby. He greeted the New Year in quaint fashion at Schloss Enzefeld, near Vienna, which had been his temporary home since he arrived from France on 14 December. On the stroke of midnight David was given a sucking pig to hold which, according to custom, would bring good luck in the year ahead.

Chapter Eleven

The Duke and Mrs Allen

Scarcely had the New Year begun than George of Kent found himself at the centre of what the press, with its ear for a good royal story, mischievously turned into a minor scandal. The episode had started in apparent innocence on 1 January. That morning, beneath headline news that Mussolini was to ban Italian volunteers from joining the Spanish Civil War, and sandwiched between a goodwill message from George VI, the engagement of tennis-star Betty Nuthall, and news of the Third Test in Melbourne, the *Daily Express* ran an entertaining feature about the visit of the Duke of Kent and a certain 'Mrs Allen' to Miss Evelyn Bool at the London Phrenological Institution at Ludgate Circus. There the Duke and his companion had their heads 'read' by the elderly Miss Bool. By feeling the contours of a person's head phrenologists claim to reveal a person's abilities and characteristics. They then prepare a chart forecasting the pursuits in which the person is most likely to succeed.

Miss Bool, who was reported to have been 'thrilled by her fifteen-minute reading of a royal head', said afterwards, that the Duke of Kent had 'A very nicely balanced head. I should say a fine quality of brain matter rather than quantity. If he were out in the world looking for a job, he would be best suited for classical or artistic work.' It was all harmless stuff and as such it might have remained, had not the *Express* asked on its front page next day, 'Who is Mrs Allen?' Under a photograph of a dark, sultry beauty, William Hickey replied:

> She is Mrs William Allen, wife of a wealthy business man who was formerly M.P. for West Belfast and is an authority

on the peoples of the Near East.

As Miss Paula Gellibrand – 'The Gellibrand' – she was London's most beautiful mannequin in 1922, and was painted by many artists. As the Marquise de Casa Maury [predecessor of Freda Dudley-Ward, who, in October 1937, married the Marquis, after divorcing her first husband] she became one of the best-known figures in the social circle in which the Duke and Duchess of Kent move.

From then on, rumours that Prince George and Mrs Allen were having an affair became widespread until, on 16 January, the *Evening Standard*'s 'Londoner's Diary' – ostensibly in an attempt to put a stop to the stories – declared that the consequences of the couple's visit to Miss Bool had been

> . . . ludicrous and – to members of the royal family and Mrs Allen – extremely painful. His Royal Highness has been the recipient of a flood of letters, most of them anonymous, describing the occasion in terms varying from crude innuendo to open accusation.
>
> Rumour's latest guise is that, in consequence of the Duke's relationship with Mrs Allen, divorce proceedings have already been instituted by her husband. . . . For the past three years Mr and Mrs 'Bill' Allen have been living almost entirely in Ireland. On one of their rare visits to London Mrs Allen, who has been a friend of the Duke's since his midshipman days, called at Belgrave Square . . . to see the Duchess and her newly-born daughter.

Within days the press tired of its own intrigue, but not before 'Bill' Allen had spoken up for himself and, via *The Times*, issued a thinly veiled threat to the perpetrators of the scandal, and indeed to other interested parties:

> In connexion with the Press persecution initiated as the result of a casual and utterly harmless visit of my wife to a phrenologist in company with a member of the royal family, I should like to record the fact in your columns that my mother-in-law, an elderly lady in weak health living alone, has been reduced to a state of nervous exhaustion by the relentless attentions of reporters. . . . I have now

arranged for her protection and a warm reception for any
further visitors.

>   If the 'liberty of the Press' in this country is to be expressed
> in the form of the persecution of individuals of all classes
> of the community . . . it is high time that measures were
> taken by Parliament to put some restraint upon a licence
> which amounts to an intolerable and ever-growing scandal.
> Otherwise certain individuals, who have grown rich upon
> the ruthless exploitation of other people's private lives, will
> find that they have come into conflict with men who are
> not in such a helpless position as some who have recently
> been tortured on the wheel of the yellow Press.

What that unhappy man might have said of the 'yellow Press'
today requires little imagination. But, while it is debatable how
much real harm is ever done by stories such as this, the 'affair'
of George and Mrs Allen was no more than a storm in a teacup.
Before long it had slipped from the public's notoriously short
memory altogether.

In its place, as spring approached, came thoughts of the forth-
coming coronation of George VI and Queen Elizabeth. About a
year before, Wednesday 12 May 1937 had been fixed for the coronation of Edward VIII and, as many of the plans were already
well advanced, it was considered inadvisable to alter the date.
After all, what, save the man about to be crowned, had changed?

On coronation morning George and Marina were up early to
put on their finery for the long day ahead. The Duke, who was
to ride behind George III's splendid state coach as part of Bertie
and Elizabeth's escort, dressed in full ceremonial naval uniform
with cocked hat. Across the left shoulder of his tail coat with
its gold-fringed epaulettes and tasselled braid he wore the ribbon
of the Order of the Garter and with it the star given to him on
his twenty-first birthday. He also wore the stars of the Order of
the Thistle and the Order of St Michael and St George.

Marina, who was once again the best dressed of all the royal
womenfolk, ranking, as Molyneux once put it, 'with the Empress
Eugénie among the world's outstanding leaders of fashion', wore
a slender gown of gold tissue, embroidered with sequinned
feathers. During the service at Westminster Abbey she sat in the
royal gallery, occupying a seat between the Duchess of Gloucester

and the Queen's mother, Lady Strathmore, while in the row behind old Princess Marie Louise peered intently at the comings and goings through a pair of lorgnettes. With the arrival of the sovereign and his consort – the King in a vaguely medieval costume; the plump little Queen in ivory satin – the long coronation ceremony, rich in feudal and religious symbolism, finally began.

Three weeks later yet another royal ceremony, this time conducted with the utmost simplicity, took place far away from the blare of fanfares and the general hullaballoo of the coronation. The event, celebrated in France at the Château de Candé, near Tours, on Thursday 3 June, was the wedding of the Duke and Duchess of Windsor. Chips Channon noted in his diary:

> Almost every newspaper . . . has run a leader of good wishes to the Duke of Windsor. 'The Times', however, refrained. It is of course an organ of the Archbishop [of Canterbury] and he is a power behind it. I think it is disgraceful. The treatment of the Duke of Windsor by the present Government has hurt the institution of royalty far more than ever the Duke of Windsor did himself by his abdication.

Younger members of the royal family felt much the same way. Echoing the thoughts of Lady Iris Mountbatten, George Lascelles, elder son of the Princess Royal, and now Earl of Harewood, recalled, '. . . it was hard for the younger among us not to stand in amazement at the moral contradiction between the elevation of code of duty on the one hand, and on the other the denial of central Christian virtues – forgiveness, understanding, family tenderness'.

Where, indeed, were 'Christian virtues' to be found within the royal family? Admittedly its members have always stood fast in *official* recognition of the Church's teachings, but *unofficially*, and in their private lives, it has often been a very different story. Where, as a supposedly devout Christian family, for instance, did they stand in their observance of the Ten Commandments? In their condemnation of the Duke of Windsor and, more particularly, in their treatment of the Duchess, most members of the royal family became party to the most appalling hypocrisy.

For some time David hoped that his brother George would go to France to act as his best man. In the circumstances that was both foolish and naïve of him. George, like Harry Gloucester, sent David and Wallis a wedding present, while Queen Mary, together with Bertie and Elizabeth, cabled their best wishes. Otherwise there was nothing – well, not quite nothing. On the eve of his wedding, David received a letter from the King, advising him that Wallis would not be granted the style and rank of Royal Highness. What that meant, in effect, was that George VI and his ministers, were giving David as Duke of Windsor something he had been denied as King – a morganatic marriage.

Though no members of the royal family attended the wedding, Bertie and Elizabeth, like George and Marina, were keen to hear all about it. Lady Alexandra Metcalfe, who had once been tipped as a possible wife for George, and whose husband 'Fruity' was equerry – and in the event, best man – to the Duke of Windsor, had been one of the guests. When she returned to London, Lady Alexandra told her royal inquisitors all they wanted to know. The subject was then dropped, never to be referred to again.

That June, Cecil Beaton, who had taken any number of photographs of the former Mrs Simpson, was invited to France to take the official wedding photographs of the Duke and his bride; Wallis was Marina's only equal in chic and sheer style. In his long career Cecil Beaton became the acknowledged master of his profession, but while the Windsors and the Duchess of Gloucester were among his many sitters, he yearned to photograph the Duchess of Kent. Marina had of course sat for several eminent photographers, notably Dorothy Wilding, Horst, Harlip and Bassano. She had also posed for portraits by such celebrated painters as Philip de Laszlo and Saveley Sorine, but Beaton had yet to receive a summons. When it finally came during the summer of 1937 Beaton was jubilant. He wrote afterwards:

> The Duchess looked excessively beautiful in a huge brown
> tulle crinoline, ruched like a Queen Anne window blind, or
> a lampshade, with old-fashioned jewellery. She looked like
> a Winterhalter painting and it was thus that she was
> photographed, slightly nervous at first and very Royal, with
> her deep, clipped accented voice, but soon she was as pliable
> as any sitter I have ever had and we made many jokes and
> got along splendidly.

In his authorized biography of Beaton, Hugo Vickers tells us that the Duke of Kent then arrived in a bad temper, and there is no one bloodier than he in a bad mood'. Cecil took some [photographs] of him in naval uniform and some of them together. A few days later he went to the Kents' house in Belgrave Square to present his work. The Duchess asked him, 'Well, and how are they?', and he went into raptures: 'Oh Ma'am, I think they're incredibly romantic. There are some as nostalgic and summer scented as if Winterhalter had painted your great-aunt Queen Mary. Some are an idyll, the feathery trees and the summer lighting are really. . . .'

The Duchess cut him short. Cecil and the Kents then selected the pictures for each magazine. 'Oh! I hate to be in the *Sketch* and *Tatler* and *Vogue*,' said the Duchess, adding, 'but *Vogue*'s a fashion magazine.' To this the Duke screwed up his nose with a laugh and said, 'Well, what about it? Aren't we fashionable?'

In July the Duke and Duchess of Kent were preparing for their summer holiday. For Marina a few days with Eddie and the seven-month-old Alexandra, at Bloody Point House, a converted coast-guard station at Shingle End near Sandwich in Kent, would precede a jaunt by car to Germany. There she and George would stay with Toto and Woolly – whose second child, Helen Marina Elisabeth, had been born that May – before visiting friends in Lancut, Poland, and ending up as usual with Paul and Olga at their home in Yugoslavia.

On 27 July, Marina, casual but as elegant as ever in a polka-dot dress, light blouson jacket, two-tone shoes and gloves, left Belgrave Square with her children for Shingle End. *En route* her car was involved in a serious collision with another. Miraculously no one was injured. Badly shaken, Marina gathered up a rug and spread it out in a field where she helped to comfort the family. The holder of a nearby coffee stall had rushed to their assistance and, at the Duchess's request, had telephoned for a relief car to fetch them.

Four months later, in a tragedy that foreshadowed one that was to occur in not dissimilar circumstances in 1942, the royal family was horrified by the loss of Marina's first cousin – and the future Duke of Edinburgh's sister – Cecile, Grand Duchess of Hesse, her husband the Grand Duke Georg Donatus, their two young sons, the dowager Grand Duchess, and two further members of their party.

Prince Louis of Hesse, younger brother of the Grand Duke, was due to be married to Margaret, daughter of Sir Auckland and Lady Geddes, at the church of St Peter's, Eaton Square on 20 November, in the presence of most of the royal family. Four days before the wedding the grand ducal party left Frankfurt to fly to Croydon Aerodrome aboard a three-engined Junkers Ju52 aircraft of Sabena Airways. At Steene, near Ostend, one hour after take-off, the plane encountered a sudden dense fog that had drifted in from the sea, and with visibility down to twenty feet, clipped the top of a brickworks chimney. One wing and an engine were torn away and the aircraft plunged in flames into the brickworks below. There were no survivors. The wedding of Prince Louis and Miss Geddes, which had already been postponed by the death of the bridegroom's father in October, was brought forward by three days and, in an atmosphere of funereal gloom, took place just after dawn on the morning of 17 November.

The following February George and Marina were on holiday at St Anton with Woolly and Toto, when they received word that the condition of Prince Nicholas, who had been unwell since mid-January, had deteriorated. Perhaps because Marina disliked flying she, Woolly and their husbands caught the night express from Munich bound for Athens. Time lost as a result of the long journey by rail meant that two of Prince Nicholas's daughters were not with him, when he died from arteriosclerosis at the Hotel Grand Bretagne, on 8 February. When, *en route*, the train stopped in Belgrade, Prince Paul was there to meet it. It was he who had the sorry task of telling Marina and Elizabeth that, during the night, Prince Nicholas's condition had grown worse and that shortly after a priest had administered Extreme Unction, he whispered to his wife and elder daughter, 'I am happy to die in my own beloved country,' and slipped into a coma.

Prince Nicholas was remembered by Chips Channon as 'A gentle, dreamy gentleman . . . particularly devoted to the late George v, who was his first cousin. To him, he was in the habit of sending naughty stories and doubtful limericks; for the late King had a racy mind and liked a vulgar joke, so long as the point was obvious.'

Upon their arrival in Athens, the Duchess of Kent and Countess

Toerring went straight to their parents' suite at the Grand Bretagne and, with their mother and sister, sat by their father's body for fifteen minutes. A few days later the sixty-five-year-old prince was buried near his parents at Tatoi. For the first five or six months of her widowhood, Princess Nicholas was taken care of by Princess Olga. Eventually, having decided to settle permanently in Athens, the Princess found a comfortable suburban villa and there, becoming increasingly eccentric and surrounded by a number of pet cats, she remained until the end of her life.

In the three years since her marriage the Duchess of Kent had accepted two presidencies: the YWCA Central Club for Women and Girls, and Alexandra Rose Day. She had also become patron of the Central School of Speech and Drama, the Elizabeth Garrett Anderson Hospital, and the Women's Holiday Fund. During the next quarter of a century she would become actively involved with another sixty-six diverse organizations, including the People's Dispensary for Sick Animals, the Royal National Lifeboat Institution, the Anglo-Hellenic League, the Chelsea Play Centre for Children, the All England Lawn Tennis Club, the Chest and Heart Association, the Old Vic and the British School in Rome. Worthy and, in some cases, vitally important though the aims of the Duchess's charities were, there was nothing especially remarkable about the nature of her presidencies or patronages, apart from the fact that her support was based on a genuine desire to be of benefit.

For his part the Duke of Kent was no less popular among the communities he served in an official capacity, trying, as he put it, 'to gain a real appreciation of this country's problems by personal contact'. It was in recognition of his brother's achievements – and, no doubt, in tribute to the days when they were called 'The Foreman' and 'The Factory Inspector' – that George VI invited the Duke of Kent to become Governor-General of Australia, in succession to Lord Gowrie.

George's appointment was to take effect from November 1939 and, to that end, he set about making enthusiastic plans: relinquishing the house in Belgrave Square; arranging to ship some of their furniture out to Government House in Canberra; and again selecting colour schemes, furnishing fabrics, and so on with which to 'revolutionize' the look of their new and even more impressive home. In her own biography of Princess Marina, Stella King wrote:

> Curtains, hangings and tailored covers without traditional
> flounces were sent from England. [The Duke] chose oatmeal-
> coloured silk tweed curtains, pale blue satin-covered sofas
> and chairs, and white Grecian rugs, which pleased the
> Duchess. The Duke also ordered £5,000 worth of household
> linen, which he paid for himself and included peach-
> coloured silk sheets edged with satin at £50 a pair.

The Australians themselves seemed delighted by the Duke of Kent's appointment. 'It is the greatest compliment the Throne can pay to the Australian people,' said the *Sydney Sun*, while at home, Winston Churchill considered it a 'master-stroke of Imperial policy'. Only Marina winced at the prospect of living so very far away from her family, in a country that was then scarcely noted for its gentility, social graces or any kind of cultural heritage. Indeed, if Australians were as eager to know her as contemporary reports suggest, Marina was hard put to return the compliment.

In the event, world affairs put an end to the Kents' plans. On 3 September, only two months before they were due to leave England, the Duchess was listening to the radio in the music room at Coppins, when it was announced that Britain was at war with Germany.

Chapter Twelve

Friends of Franklin D.

At the outbreak of the Second World War George, Duke of Kent was back in naval uniform once more. This time, however, it was not the kind of Gilbert and Sullivan costume tinkling with stars, orders and token medals, so beloved of kings and princes, but the sober rig of an officer reporting for desk duty at the Admiralty.

Unlikely though it seems of a man who could not wait to be free of a *bona fide* service career only ten years earlier, claims have been made that George would have liked to have gone to war in command of his own ship. The very thought is preposterous. Yet all the same, it was not long before George vi's youngest brother – whose consolation prize for not having gone to Australia was 'promotion' to the rank of Rear-Admiral – wanted to do something more than sit in an office overlooking Horse Guards Parade. Thus, as history repeated itself, the King agreed to George's transfer to the Royal Air Force with the spurious rank of Air Vice-Marshal. To a large extent, the Duke of Kent's duties in the RAF reflected the work he had undertaken for the Home Office Factory Inspectorate, though the emphasis had now been shifted from overseeing safety regulations and working conditions to boosting workers' morale. In the performance of these duties, George dropped the rank conferred on him by the King, in favour of that of Group Captain. The reason for this was simply to prevent him from being placed in a superior position to those officers under whom he would have to work.

In the meantime, Marina had also joined the Navy as Commandant of the Women's Royal Naval Service – the Wrens. Jennifer Ellis wrote:

She was the most conscientious of Commandants, and the post was anything but a nominal one. She travelled all over the country, visiting all the chief centres of the WRNS, never sparing herself a tiring or difficult journey. She brought a human touch to even a routine inspection. Walking down a line of girls, she would stop to talk to each one personally, not just a conventional sentence or two, but with genuine interest.

As far as the women's services were concerned, Marina did more for the image and morale of the Wrens than any costly promotion campaign. 'Every time her photo appeared in the press in her . . . uniform', recalled Dame Vera Laughton Matthews, then Director of the WRNS, 'there was a rush to join up.' The Duchess also had a hand in the design of the uniform she wore to such dramatic effect; that is to say, she, the Director and the First Lord of the Admiralty put their heads together over a change in the style of hat to be worn by the Wrens. 'It's very important to recruiting,' Marina said. 'No woman wants to wear a hat that makes her look unattractive, war or no war.'

From the time of her appointment right through to the declaration of peace five years later, Marina's personal touch never failed to weave a spell that was nothing short of inspirational. Dame Vera Laughton Matthews said,

> Wherever she went on her tours of inspection she gave enormous pleasure. She insisted on seeing the girls' quarters, and on finding out whether they were comfortable. She visited the galleys and talked to the cooks. Young people are always quick to recognize sincerity. The girls felt that the Duchess took a personal interest in them, and that she really cared whether they were happy or not.

It was in that spirit of personal involvement that the Duchess of Kent agreed to appeal for yet more recruits. That broadcast which, in the words of the Director of the WRNS, brought 'an immediate response from all over the country', was transmitted on 20 January 1941. This is what Marina said:

> Since February 1940, when I became Commandant of the Women's Royal Naval Service, I have been able to visit a number of ports where units of the Wrens are employed.

I had always heard what a wonderful spirit of friendship existed throughout the organization. As a result of my visits, I know this was no exaggeration and I also know why. Wren officers are promoted from the ranks and so they understand the conditions of life and work among the ratings with whom they have to deal. During last year, an average of thirty ratings a month were made officers. About one-third of them are responsible for welfare and discipline. They are chosen because of their abilities as leaders and because of their experience in looking after the well-being of other people.

In the Wren organization, particular care is taken also to provide comfortable quarters and good food. From my own experience, I can tell you how good it is. The remaining two-thirds of the officers are employed on duties which would otherwise be performed by naval officers; such as cyphering or secretarial and confidential work. This enables officers to be released for more active duties with the Fleet. I feel sure that there are still many women who would like to do their bit by helping the Royal Navy, the traditional service of the empire.

So far I have talked only about officers, because all who join the Wrens have an opportunity of being promoted as the occasion arises. But when you first join there are plenty of opportunities and much interesting and useful work to be done.

The Navy has to be fed, and cooks and stewards are wanted, particularly in the big training establishments for the Navy and the Fleet Air Arm. Ledger clerks and book-keepers are also needed as accounts have to be kept. Morse has to be transcribed by wireless telegraphists; messages have to be taken by telephone operators; signals teleprinted and records kept. Shorthand typists are also wanted.

Many of you, I know, would like to help the Navy in these ways, but on account of lack of training or experience, perhaps you feel that you cannot do so. There are, however, some categories where a little training can be turned to good account. If you can cook but have no professional experience, the Women's Royal Naval Service will train you. Many Wren cooks are being trained at the Royal Naval

cookery schools. If you like household duties, the Wrens can
make you a first-class steward. It may mean a sacrifice to
leave your home and possibly work which interests you, but
you will have the feeling that your new work is essential
to our war effort. In this connection, I should like to say
a word of congratulation to the many thousands of Wrens
who are already serving their country. We are very proud
of the wonderful way in which you have carried on your
work during air raids and at times of tension. We admire
your courage and we know that danger is met unflinchingly,
because the future happiness of our families and homes
depends on victory. If you join the Wrens, you will know
that you have done your share and are worthy of your country.

The Navy was not the Duchess of Kent's only wartime involvement. At the very start she offered her services to the Iver and
Denham Cottage Hospital, which she had opened a few years
earlier, and there, along with several other local volunteers, she
made dressings, splints, swabs, and helped generally. Later on
she went to work at University College Hospital, London as a
nursing auxiliary.

At the time, a Miss Bond was Sister of Ward 16. She recalled:
'. . . the Matron sent for me one day and told me that the Duchess
of Kent was to work on my ward. . . . She was to be known as
Nurse Kay and her identity was to be a close secret. The Registrar
and Senior Surgeon obviously knew what was afoot but the news
didn't leak out for the first few weeks.' That it did leak out sooner
than anybody might have wished was due to a vigilant patient,
a dressmaker's assistant, who naturally kept a close watch on
the fashion columns. Having been fobbed off with repeated assur-
ances that the royal lookalike was only 'Nurse Kay', the patient
finally declared triumphantly, 'That VAD* *is* the Duchess of Kent.
I've seen her pictures dozens of times. Nobody is going to tell
me it isn't her.'

During her 'anonymous' period at the hospital, of which she
became Patron in 1942, Princess Marina

> . . . came and went as much as she liked – or as official
> commitments would permit. She took part in all routine

---

* Voluntary Aid Detachment – a volunteer military nurse.

activities in the ward – surgical dressings, bedmaking, washing patients, doing hair, tidying lockers, plumping up pillows, feeding and handing round meals on trays. She assisted in the pre-operational preparation of patients who were due for the theatre . . . and the removal of tubes after the operations was also part of her job.

In common with the comings and goings of the rest of the royal family, news of the wartime engagements of both the Duke and the Duchess of Kent was carefully censored. Visits to factories, air raid precautions depots, hospitals, rest centres, fire stations and so on were never broadcast in advance, and press items that appeared afterwards only ever gave the sketchiest details. According to James Wentworth-Day, the Duke of Kent

> . . . went down to the East End dozens of times whilst air raids were on and was in one shelter, holding no less than 7,000 people whilst the place shuddered to bomb-blast. Once a time bomb blew up with a terrific explosion within yards of his car. Bricks, broken glass and debris rained down. The Duke stopped his car, got out, perfectly unperturbed, walked across to a group of people, and said, 'That was a near thing, wasn't it? I am very glad to see that none of you are hurt.'

One particularly delicate mission entrusted to the Duke of Kent at this time called for all the charm, warmth and diplomacy at his command. In June 1940 Winston Churchill selected him to fly to Portugal to call upon the Prime Minister, Dr Antonio Salazar. Though ostensibly heading the British delegation attending the 800th anniversary celebrations of Portuguese independence, the true purpose of the Duke's mission was twofold. First it was to reaffirm the historic friendship that had existed between Britain and Portugal since the fourteenth century, and second, to reassure the strictly neutral Salazar that Britain's position in the war was not the lost cause German propaganda would have him believe. Prince George returned to London on 2 July, secure in the knowledge that the sympathies of the Portuguese dictator were with Britain and the Allies; while Churchill, in entrusting the task to the Duke of Kent, chalked up another victory.

The following year George, newly promoted to the rank of Air

Commodore, undertook yet another goodwill mission. This time, since it was already agreed that he should visit Canada from late July to early September in order to inspect air training schools, George suggested that he might slip in a visit to his friends the Roosevelts. Not only would it be an important diplomatic gesture – a personal thank you from the King's brother for American aid – but it would also provide him with an opportunity of seeing something of American factories engaged in the war effort.

The Duke's idea was approved in London and the proposal was put forward to Lord Halifax, Britain's Ambassador in Washington. From his office on 24 July 1941 a letter was sent to the President informing him of the purpose of the Duke of Kent's tour of Canada, and adding that

> His Royal Highness . . . would very much like to take the opportunity of paying a visit of courtesy to you. . . . It has also been suggested that the Duke while in the United States might visit one of the dockyards engaged in repairing a British warship, and possibly a factory producing aircraft for Great Britain.

On 2 August President Roosevelt approved the schedule for the Duke of Kent's three-day visit, which was arranged to take place from 23 to 26 August. Three weeks later, attended by John Lowther, his private secretary; Wing-Commander Sir Louis Greig; and Inspector James Evans of Scotland Yard, the Duke's personal detective, George flew into New York's La Guardia airport. For the first thirty-six hours of his visit the Duke relaxed with Franklin and Eleanor Roosevelt at Hyde Park, their family home in New York State, before accompanying the President to Washington and the start of more formal activities.

On Monday 25 August, Prince George flew to Norfolk in Virginia, to visit the National Advisory Committee for Aeronautics laboratory; the following day he flew to Baltimore where he inspected the Glenn Martin aircraft factory, addressed the 10,000-strong workforce, and took lunch in the Junior Executives' dining room. Back in Washington early that evening, George and his party toured the Capitol, the Supreme Court, the Washington Monument and the Lincoln Memorial, before visiting the Mellon Art Gallery, attending a cocktail party given by the National Press Club, and meeting Dominion ministers at the British Embassy.

After the Duke's visit Eleanor Roosevelt said, 'I think what impresses me most of all in meeting English people today is the great strain under which they have been and their sense of obligation in fulfilling whatever they consider is their duty. In coming to Canada and the United States, they represent the British people and they try in every way to express to us the appreciation they feel for the constant flow of aid from this country.'

In a cable to the Roosevelts which he sent from Hamilton, Ontario the day after he returned to Canada, the Duke of Kent reinforced that message when he said:

> On leaving your country I would like to thank you, Mr President and Mrs Roosevelt, once again for your wonderful kindness and hospitality during my stay. I am deeply appreciative of the opportunity which was given to me to see something of what your country is doing to help Britain and I am greatly impressed with what is being done and what can be done.

From The Citadel in Quebec on 5 September George reiterated his thanks in more personal letters to both Franklin and Eleanor Roosevelt. Addressing himself to the President, the Duke, in his stylish and distinctive hand, wrote:

> I waited until my arrival here before writing to you to thank you once more for all your kindness . . . during my visit to USA. I cannot thank you enough for having me to stop with you & for giving me the opportunity of talking to you & hearing your views on so many subjects. The gratitude of the British people for what you have done for us is immeasurable – & their admiration is unbounded – but I feel I must add my own word of admiration for all you are doing. . . . I was so glad to see something of your forces & also of the naval & air force plants. The Glenn Martin factory is most impressive – I am only sorry my stay was so short & that I was unable to see more.
>
> I have had a very rushed trip since I left Washington & only arrived here yesterday to stay with the Athlones [his uncle the Earl of Athlone, who was Governor-General of Canada from 1940 to 1946, and Princess Alice]. I leave for England some time next week & shall take back to the King

not only many messages from you but also many heartening words of all I have seen in your country.

Between their official duties George and Marina tried to preserve some sense of normality in what, during the war years, passed for home life. As parents, both the Duke and the Duchess of Kent were devoted to Eddie and Alexandra; scuttling home in time for the children's tea on days when they had public engagements to perform, playing games, telling bedtime stories, showing them off to friends, and savouring the small incidents and childish sayings beloved of most parents. At the age of five or six, Eddie had already started to show signs of the Duke's love of cars and all things mechanical, and at Coppins father and son would spend hours tinkering about in the garage. To the young prince, the Duke was also the fount of all knowledge, and there is a story that when he was in hospital having his tonsils out, Eddie asked his mother, 'How many bricks are there in the hospital, Mummy?' Marina confessed she hadn't a clue nor, when asked, had the Matron, of course. A little later, the boy proudly proclaimed that his father had solved the mystery. Greatly impressed, but nevertheless curious, the Matron took the Duke aside and asked him how he had discovered the answer. 'I didn't,' he replied, 'but for heaven's sake don't tell my son that I'm a liar.'

Like most children, Prince Edward and his sister were boisterous and inevitably clumsy. At the end of one visit to the family, Chips Channon recorded:

> . . . afternoon tea ended in tragedy as Little Edward became bumptious and knocked over a table, spilling a kettle of hot water over his little pink legs. . . . The Duke lost his temper, the Duchess was in a flurry, nannies rushed in, but little Alexandra, delightfully unconcerned, turned round, and as if to change the subject said, 'I love soldiers, do you?'

The Kents' third child and second son was born at Coppins at 7.35 pm on Saturday 4 July 1942. For once, the Home Secretary – traditionally present at a royal birth, or at least in the next room – was absent. The then incumbent, Herbert Morrison, was too tied up with extra duties as Minister of Home Security to waste time observing the niceties of a custom originally instituted in 1688 to ensure that changelings were not slipped into royal cradles.

Vastly out of date though it was, the tradition was not abolished until 1948, when Princess Elizabeth was expecting the birth of the present Prince of Wales. Six years earlier the Home Secretary had simply to accept the Duke of Kent's word that the latest addition to his family was indeed a legitimate member of the Royal House of Windsor.

With the birth of their younger son having come on a day of such national importance in the United States, George and Marina decided to ask Franklin Roosevelt to act as one of the godparents. Two days later their invitation was formally extended to the President via John Winant, then American Ambassador in London, who cabled Washington: 'The Duke of Kent has just sent me the following note. "My wife and I would be so delighted if you would be godfather to our son. We should be especially pleased, as he was born on Independence Day."' On 11 July Roosevelt responded, 'I am much thrilled and very proud to be Godfather to the youngster and I send him my affectionate greetings. Tell the Duchess that I count on seeing him as soon as the going is good.'

This rather curious form of communication between friends continued just over a fortnight later on 28 July, when Ambassador Winant sent a telegram to the President, marked 'Triple Priority'. It read: 'The Duke of Kent has asked me to send you the following message: "We are so pleased you are to be Godfather. Christening takes place August 4th at Windsor Castle. The King will stand proxy for you."' On the day of the ceremony itself the President cabled the Duke: 'My affectionate regards to Michael George Charles Franklin. I am anxious to see him as soon as I can. Do send me his photograph. Tell the King that I will hold him to strict accountability until I am able to take over the responsibility of a godfather myself. My warm regards to you and the Duchess. Franklin D. Roosevelt.'

Until the end of the war, which in 1942 still lay three years distant, family happiness for Marina, her sisters, and their sixty-year-old mother was clouded by a state of enforced separation. Woolly and her Bavarian husband Count Toerring were officially Britain's enemies; Princess Nicholas lived under German occupation in her suburban villa outside Athens; while Olga and Paul were banished to Kenya, where they were put under house arrest for alleged treason.

This is not the place for a lengthy dissertation on Yugoslav politics but, briefly, Prince Paul's fall from grace came about in March 1941 when, by yielding to ever-increasing pressure from Germany and her allies, he was forced into signing a Tripartite Pact which, in essence, guaranteed Yugoslavia freedom from attack as long as German troops and equipment were allowed free passage through to Greece. Despite an overwhelming vote in favour of this move from within the Yugoslav Cabinet itself, Prince Paul – a regent with 'too many neighbours and too few friends', as he was later described – was branded a traitor and quisling. Exile followed, and in April 1941 Prince and Princess Paul, now regarded as political prisoners, were *en route* to Kenya. There, under British jurisdiction, they were to be held at a house called Osserian near Lake Naivasha, once the home of the murdered Earl of Erroll. It was a harsh penalty for a man whose sympathies had always been fiercely pro-British and who, as regent, had attempted to steer a course that was in line with the country he admired so profoundly. But for the Duchess of Kent the defamatory speeches in the House of Commons, and the attacks upon her sister and brother-in-law published in the British press, were no less difficult to bear.

Throughout the war, communication with her mother and sisters was difficult, but not altogether impossible. Even so, there were times when Marina felt acutely lonely without the kind of intimate companionship she, Olga and Elizabeth had shared for more than thirty years. For a while, however, the Duchess had her husband in whom to find comfort and support.

Chapter Thirteen

A Tragic Mystery

Between 25 August 1941, when he visited the NACA laboratory in Norfolk, Virginia, and his death exactly one year later, the Duke of Kent had flown more than 60,000 miles on active service with the Royal Air Force. Another 1,800 miles would have been added to his record, had his scheduled mission to inspect RAF bases in Iceland been accomplished according to plan.

For the Duke and Duchess much of August had been taken up, one way and another, with family events. On the fourth, their one-month-old son Michael was christened in the private chapel at Windsor Castle, and it had been arranged that Cecil Beaton should visit Coppins on the fifteenth to take photographs of the proud parents with the baby prince. Two days before that, Queen Mary had driven over from Badminton, her home during the war, to spend the afternoon with George and Marina. The visit gave the old Queen enormous pleasure. She noted in her diary, 'The baby is sweet – Had luncheon & tea there – Walked in the garden – Georgie showed me some of his interesting things . . . he looked so happy with his lovely wife & the dear baby.'

Not quite a fortnight later, George, his private secretary Lieutenant John Lowther, his equerry Pilot Officer the Hon. Michael Strutt, and his valet Leading Aircraftman John Hales prepared themselves for the visit to Iceland. During the late afternoon of Monday 24 August the Duke said farewell to Marina before driving himself up to London, where he boarded the overnight train for Inverness.

The following morning George was met at the railway station by Group Captain Geoffrey Francis, Commanding Officer No.

4 (Coastal) Operational Training Unit at Invergordon, the Duke's point of departure. When he arrived at the base, George was introduced to the carefully selected team responsible for flying him to 'the frozen north', as he referred to his destination.

Leading the immensely experienced crew was Flight Lieutenant Frank McKenzie Goyen. A young Australian who had already flown Sir Stafford Cripps to Moscow, he had nearly 1,000 flying hours on ocean patrols to his credit. As captain, Goyen would fly the lumbering Sunderland flying boat W4026 DQ-M, which had been flown from Oban the previous weekend and was now moored on the Cromarty Firth, the surface of which looked as smooth as grey slate, as one observer described it that day. Sitting next to Goyen on the flight and acting as first pilot would be Wing Commander T.L.Moseley, Commanding Officer of 228 Squadron, attached temporarily to the Sunderland's flight crew as a courtesy to the aircraft's royal passenger. Completing the crew were Pilot Officer S.W.Smith, second pilot; Pilot Officer G.R.Saunders, acting as Navigator; Flight Sergeants C.N.Lewis, W.R.Jones and E.J.Hewerdine, and Sergeants E.F.Blacklock, A.R.Catt and L.E.Sweett. Flight Sergeant Andrew Jack was to act as rear gunner.

On 25 August, while the crew were being briefed, the Duke of Kent and his party took luncheon with Group Captain Francis. At about 12.30 pm they were ferried out to the aircraft by marine tender. Once aboard, they spent the next half hour or so making the routine pre-flight checks of instruments, and generally warming the flying boat up ready for take-off. At about one o'clock the Duke was welcomed aboard, and it is thought most likely that he and his staff would have gone straight to the wardroom in the belly of the aircraft. Minutes later the Sunderland began to move across the waters of the Cromarty Firth, which were so calm that the flying-boat needed an unusually long run before finding a wave to help it lift off. Low cloud along the south coast of Caithness that day meant that flying conditions would be poor for the first part of the flight, but the general forecast was favourable with clearer weather expected to the north and out over the Atlantic.

At 1.10 pm the Sunderland was airborne and, flying between the Sutors at the mouth of the Cromarty Firth, turned north-east to follow the coastline. Inland from the east coast village of Berriedale, no more than thirty minutes later, David Morrison and his son Hugh were rounding up their flock of sheep when they heard the aircraft approach from the sea; though because of the dense mist – known in Scotland as 'haar' – neither father nor son were able to see it. Then followed the sound of an almighty explosion as the Sunderland crashed on a hillside and two and a half thousand gallons of aviation fuel blew up, sending a wall of flame skyward. Of the fifteen men on board, all but one was killed. The single, badly burnt survivor was Andrew Jack, whose rear gun turret – ironically considered the most dangerous place to be – had broken off, hurling him to the ground.

In the past several writers seem to have been under the common misapprehension that the Sunderland collided with Eagle's Rock, an 800-foot promontory on the Duke of Portland's Langwell estate. Others have claimed that it cleared the summit of the rock, but ploughed into rising ground beyond. Neither assumption is correct. For the aircraft to have encountered Eagle's Rock at all, it would have had to have approached the hill from a different direction altogether, probably consistent with flying towards, not away from, Invergordon. What the Sunderland had in fact cleared, or had perhaps flown round, was the 2,000-foot summit of Meall Dhonuill, or Donald's Mount, situated at the eastern end of Scaraben, a ridge running east to west and lying south of Eagle's Rock itself. Having cleared Donald's Mount, however and, for some inexplicable reason in thick mist and hazardous terrain, the plane descended to an altitude of only 700 feet and thundered straight into the gently sloping hill which, at its western extreme, rises to Eagle's Rock.

At the sound of the explosion, Hugh Morrison sprinted downhill to the track where he had left his motorcycle and sped to the little community of Braemore to raise the alarm. He then rode on to the coastal village of Dunbeath to alert the local physician, Dr Kennedy, and the police. Immediately the first search party set out from Braemore, north-east of the site of the crash, while crofters and ghillies, who had also heard the news, set out from Berriedale. Later that afternoon the search parties discovered the wreckage and the bodies. From his house in Dunbeath, the elderly Dr Kennedy and two special constables, one of whom was William Bethune, hastened to the scene. Both Kennedy and Bethune identified the Duke of Kent's body, which, still clad in his flying suit, had been flung clear of the wreckage. Despite a severe gash to the head, his features were still clearly discernible, though the inscription on his identity bracelet dispelled any doubt. It read: 'His Royal Highness The Duke of Kent, "The Coppins", Iver, Buckinghamshire'.

That evening at Coppins, when the telephone rang, Marina had not long gone to her bedroom, intending to have an early night. Kate Fox, who had nursed the Duchess as a baby thirty-six years earlier, and who had come out of retirement to help with the now seven-week-old Prince Michael, took the call. Numb with shock, and perhaps wondering just how best to break the news, she slowly climbed the stairs. Hearing her, it is said that Marina immediately sensed catastrophe, and the moment Foxy opened the door, she cried out, 'It's George, isn't it?'

At Balmoral the King and Queen were having dinner with Harry and Alice, the Duke and Duchess of Gloucester, when the steward entered the dining room and whispered to the King that Sir Archibald Sinclair, Secretary of State for Air, was on the telephone and needed to speak to him urgently. When he rejoined his family, George VI was grim-faced and silent. The news, he wrote, 'came as a great shock to me, & I had to break it to Elizabeth, & Harry & Alice who were staying with us. ... We left Balmoral in the evening for London.'

When the King was called from the table, the Duchess of Gloucester's first thoughts were of Queen Mary – that something had happened to her. In fact the Queen Dowager had spent the day in active high spirits. During the morning she had driven over to Corsham Court, home of Lord Methuen, to attend a lecture and admire the picture gallery; had spent the rest of that wet afternoon at Badminton, putting photographs into her huge scarlet folio albums; and after tea had sat at her needlework, while Lady Cynthia Colville, one of her ladies-in-waiting, read to her. News of Georgie's death was received shortly after dinner. 'I felt so stunned by the shock', Queen Mary wrote in her diary, 'I could not believe it.' The following morning the Queen climbed into her famous old Daimler and drove to Coppins. When she arrived, she found Marina in a pitifully desolate state; one moment sobbing uncontrollably, the next staring blankly into space, utterly motionless.

As the disaster made headline news around the world, tributes

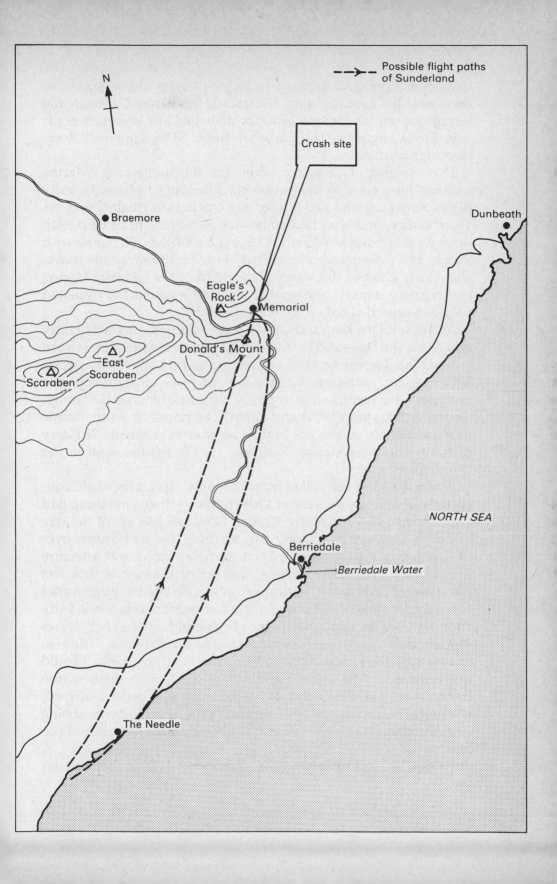

to the Duke poured in. From Australia, where Parliament was adjourned as a mark of respect, Premier Curtin said that Australians 'had always highly regarded the Duke, whose designation for the Governor-Generalship had evoked real pleasure'. In Victoria, the Greek community prepared a message of condolence for the Duchess, in which they expressed their appreciation of the fact that Prince George had been a 'staunch supporter of our beloved and suffering country'. From Canada, Prime Minister Mackenzie King said of the Duke, 'I greatly admired him for his public service and his attractive personality.' Further tributes were received from the Presidents and Prime Ministers of New Zealand, South Africa, Portugal, Argentina and China, while in the United States Senator Connolly, Chairman of the Senate Foreign Relations Committee said, 'The Duke of Kent's brave conduct will serve as an inspiration to his gallant comrades in the armies and navies of the United Nations.'

More private messages were sent to the royal family by those who had ties of personal friendship. In a telegram to the widowed Duchess President Roosevelt said, 'I am shocked beyond measure at hearing of the tragic accident and I want you to know that I feel the loss very deeply and personally. He has given his life for his Nation and in a great cause. I am thinking much of you and the babies.'

In response, Marina wired, 'Am deeply touched by your kind and understanding sympathy and your appreciation of my beloved husband. Am heartbroken.'

To Queen Mary, Roosevelt cabled, 'May I tell you of my great sorrow in hearing of the tragic accident to your gallant boy'; while to the King, his message read, 'I feel that I have lost an old and true friend and I want you to know how heartsick I am at this tragic accident. My wife and I are thinking much of all of you.'

Other friends were no less stunned. Noël Coward, who had reasons enough for remembering the Duke with particular affection, wrote in his diary on 26 August:

A dreadful morning. Headlines in the papers saying that the Duke of Kent was killed yesterday afternoon in an air crash. I can hardly believe it, but of course that is nonsense because I believe it only too well. It is never difficult to believe that someone young and charming and kind is dead. They are always dying. . . . Well, there goes a friendship of nineteen years. I shall miss him most horribly. He may have had his faults, but he was kind always and I feel absolutely miserable. . . . I am taking this resentfully and personally. I am so deeply sorry for the poor Duchess. I wrote to her this morning, of course, a rather inarticulate letter. . . . In memoriam I say, 'Thank you for your friendship for me over all these years and I shall never forget you.'

In Scotland on 27 August the body of the thirty-nine-year-old Duke, contained in an oak coffin draped with the blue flag of the RAF, was taken from Dunrobin Castle, seat of the Duke of Sutherland, where aircraftmen had mounted an all-night vigil, to the local railway station. There the London-bound train made an extra stop and, as the guard of honour presented arms, and a crowd of local people wept openly, the coffin was borne to a special carriage and placed next to those of some of the Sunderland's other victims. Later that day the Duke's remains were conveyed by road from Euston Station to Windsor Castle, where they were solemnly placed in the sumptuous, yet almost too ornate Albert Memorial Chapel, wherein lie the tombs of Queen Mary's first fiancé, the Duke of Clarence, and Queen Victoria's youngest son Leopold, Duke of Albany.

When Marina arrived at the chapel shortly afterwards, clutching a small bunch of red and white roses which she had cut from bushes grown by the Duke at Coppins, she asked to be left entirely alone. Outside in the Galilee Porch, a stone passage that separates the Albert Memorial Chapel from the body of St George's Chapel, the Duchess's lady-in-waiting, Lady Herbert, stood quietly with officers of the Grenadier Guards. Fifteen minutes later, having said her private farewell, Marina re-emerged. Next day she returned once more, a solitary black-clad figure in the midst of a mass of colour – the floor paved with veined marbles of various hue, the walls painted with biblical scenes, the vaulted roof gilded and set with Venetian glass mosaic; all outward expressions of an earlier inconsolable grief, that of Queen Victoria for her husband Albert, the Prince Consort.

The funeral of Prince George, Duke of Kent, took place in St George's Chapel on the morning of Saturday 29 August. Supported by the Queen and Queen Mary, Marina, now heavily veiled, was conducted to her place opposite the purple catafalque near the high altar. Minutes later, having come from the Albert Memorial Chapel, the cortège entered St George's to the hymn 'Abide with Me'. Now draped with the Duke of Kent's personal standard, on which was placed his Air Commodore's cap, together with his widow's wreath of multi-coloured garden flowers arranged on a base of George's favourite clove carnations, the coffin was borne in on the shoulders of four Air Vice-Marshals and two Air Marshals. Preceded by the Dean of Windsor, Dr Baillie, and by Lieutenant-Colonel Humphrey Butler and Captain Lord Herbert – who carried the Duke's insignia on crimson velvet cushions – the procession made its way along the nave and into the quire.

As it approached, Marina's gaze never left her husband's gold-braided cap until the coffin was set down on the catafalque. At that point she sank to her knees in prayer, and but for the moment when the Duke's titles were proclaimed by Garter King of Arms, she remained kneeling throughout the service. At the end, the Queen held Marina's arm as she paused to look down into the open space through which her husband's coffin had just descended. Then, as the organ played Chopin's *Funeral March*, followed by Christian Sinding's *Intermezzo No. 1*, a favourite piece of the Duke's, Marina was led from St George's.

'I have attended very many family funerals in the Chapel,' wrote King George VI 'but none ... have moved me in the same way. ...'

For Noël Coward:

> The service was impressive and supremely dignified. I tried hard not to cry, but it was useless. When the Duchess came in ... I broke a bit, and when the coffin passed with flowers from the garden at Coppins and Prince George's cap on it I was finished. ...
>
> After it was all over and the King had sprinkled the earth and the Royalties had gone away, we all went up one by one to the vault and bowed and secretly said goodbye to him. Then we went out into the very strong sunlight. Margot Oxford [Countess of Oxford and Asquith] came up to me and said, 'Very well done, wasn't it?' as though she had been at a successful first night. I thought this offensive and unforgivable.

By the time Queen Mary left Windsor to drive back to Badminton that afternoon, 'a fearful thunderstorm' had broken. Yet for that grand old dowager, the journey was not without diversion and, for a moment, her private sorrow was interrupted when she gave a lift – as she often did – to 'a charming young American parachutist', who was 'most friendly', and to 'a nice Sergeant Observer' from the Royal Air Force. Within a few days, Queen Mary had resumed what she called her 'wooding' activities, which meant sawing up logs and even trees in the grounds surrounding Badminton House. 'I am so glad I can take up my occupations again,' she wrote, 'Georgie wld have wished me to do so.'

On 14 September, three weeks after the disaster, George VI drove from Balmoral to Berriedale to visit the site of his brother's death. By the time of his arrival most of the wreckage had already been removed, perhaps out of respect to the King or to keep the press and mawkish souvenir hunters at bay. But only time and nature could erase every sign of the aircraft's devastating path. After making his 'Pilgrimage', as he described it, the King wrote: '. . . the ground for 200 yds long & 100 yds wide had been scored and scorched by its trail & by flame. It hit one side of the slope, turned over in the air & slid down the other side on its back. The impact must have been terrific as the aircraft as an aircraft was unrecognisable when found.'

What exactly happened on the afternoon of Tuesday, 25 August 1942, some thirty minutes after take-off, remains one of the greatest mysteries in aviation history. Despite the fact that George was one of the most important public figures to die in a wartime air crash, a full explanation of the tragedy has never emerged and the same baffling question inevitably confronts those who probe the disaster. How could such an experienced crew at their most alert have made such a fatal error as to descend into low cloud when the established procedure under such conditions was to gain altitude?

Among those who have made an in-depth study of the crash and its possible causes is the writer and broadcaster Robin Macwhirter. During the course of investigations for his 1985 radio programme *The Crash of W4026*, Mr Macwhirter interviewed a number of people who remembered the disaster or were in some way connected with it. These included Hugh Morrison, William Bethune and Jean Auld, a sister of the survivor, Andrew Jack.

He subsequently met Group Captain Francis, who had been Commanding Officer at Invergordon. Robin MacWhirter was to discover that all documentation pertaining to the official Court of Inquiry has apparently vanished into thin air. The Public Record Office, the RAF Historical Branch, and the Royal Archives at Windsor Castle all deny having possession of the key records that relate directly to the death of the Duke of Kent, brother of the King, and at that time fifth in line to the throne. It was also discovered that *Hansard*, in which an extract from the Court of Inquiry's findings was published, entered the date of the disaster as 15 August instead of the twenty-fifth (though that would seem to have been no more than a typographical error); and that the Record Book of 228 Squadron Coastal Command, to which the flying boat belonged, put the approximate time of the crash at 2 pm, an implausible half hour too late.

To compound the mystery still further, the discovery that the flight briefing has also disappeared, apparently without trace, means that the route Flight Lieutenant Goyen and Wing Commander Moseley were instructed to follow is open to conjecture. In an article published in the quarterly review *After the Battle*, David J. Smith, like Ralph Barker, author of *Great Mysteries of the Air*, points to the Sunderland having been instructed to take what might seem to be the most obvious route; that is to say, to follow the coastline in a north-easterly direction for some eighty to eighty-five miles, keeping out over the North Sea and turning through the Pentland Firth, on course for Reykjavik. This, however, is by no means the only route the fated Sunderland may have been told to take. RAF personnel have explained that it was far from unusual for aircraft to gain a safe altitude of 4,000 feet over the Moray Firth, then turn inland at Dunbeath to fly over the predominantly flat landscape of Caithness to the Pentland Firth. Having spoken to local people who remember the accident, Robin Macwhirter suggests that the Duke of Kent's aircraft flew up the coast and crossed inland at a point known as The Needle, just south of the Berriedale Water, and then flew up the wide river valley. It then cleared Donald's Mount at the eastern end of Scaraben and was heading north for the Pentland Firth when disaster struck.

Many theories about the cause of the crash itself and why the flying boat should have been as low as 700 feet at the time of impact have been submitted through the years. These range from the effects of down-draught on the aircraft or the influence of magnetic rocks on its compasses to plain sabotage. Some of the suggestions seemed plausible enough, albeit briefly, while others were no more than pure fantasy. None, however, has withstood the test of being scrutinized in a strong light.

On 7 October 1942, Sir Archibald Sinclair, the Secretary of State for Air, reported the findings of the special Court of Inquiry to the House of Commons. According to the extract published in *Hansard*,

> The Court found: First, that the accident occurred because the aircraft was flown on a track other than that indicated in the flight plan given to the pilot, and at too low an altitude to clear the rising ground on the track; secondly, that the responsibility for this serious mistake in airmanship lies with the captain of the aircraft; thirdly, that the weather encountered should have presented no difficulties to an experienced pilot; fourthly, that the examination of the propellors showed that the engines were under power when the aircraft struck the ground, and fifthly . . . that all the occupants of the aircraft were on duty at the time of the accident.

In his article 'The Tragedy at Eagle's Rock', published in *The Scotsman* to coincide with the BBC radio programme, Robin Macwhirter responded:

> If skipper Frank Goyen made such an elementary error as failing to seek altitude in bad visibility he wasn't alone in making that decision. Wing Commander T. L. Moseley, the CO of 228 Squadron, was seated beside him as first pilot for this special trip. Goyen also had a second pilot, a navigator and seven other men, engineers, radio operators, gunners watching what he was doing. All were men of experience, all men who valued their lives.

Chapter Fourteen

Min, Eddie, Pud & Maow

In its initial stages, the intensity of Marina's grief at Prince George's death was so great that it caused much concern within the royal family. In their own way both the King and the Queen did what they could to comfort the disconsolate widow. So, indeed, did Queen Mary, difficult though it was for her to show her feelings or release emotion, except when she expressed it on paper.

All attempts to reach the Duchess in her misery, however, were impeded by the palpable sense of distance that always existed between Marina and her husband's family – and for which Marina herself was entirely responsible. Her acute awareness of who she was, not just as Duchess of Kent, but as a thoroughbred princess of both royal and *imperial* descent in her own right, meant that she exuded a distinct air of superiority. As a result, she was never properly absorbed into the British royal family who, to quote Kenneth Rose, 'did not share her consciousness of royalty as a caste apart, or of a Europe composed more of dynasties than of nations'.

None of this is intended to imply that Marina – despite her resentment of 'those common little Scottish girls', as she referred to Queen Elizabeth and the Duchess of Gloucester – was not warmly regarded by the royal family. It was simply that through the divisive influences of background, intellect and cultivation, Marina never felt particularly close to any of her in-laws. Now, without George, the divisions between them became even more pronounced.

Impotent to penetrate the mournful shadows surrounding the grieving Duchess and spurred by compassion, King George VI performed an act of great charity. Though he anticipated a backlash, as much from within parliamentary circles as from the national press, the King realized that Marina needed to be comforted by a member of her own family. Thus, with the full approval of the Prime Minister, Winston Churchill, he cabled Princess Paul in Kenya, inviting her to come to England. On 10 September, accompanied by Mrs Lilia Ralli, an old friend of both Marina and herself, Olga set out on a journey that took her through Uganda, the Cameroons, Nigeria, and the West African coast to Portugal. From there she travelled to Ireland, thence to Poole Harbour in Dorset. On 17 September Princess Olga arrived at Coppins. It was the first time that she and Marina had seen one another for more than two years and, given the extraordinary circumstances of their meeting, it proved an intensely emotional reunion. For Marina it was also the first step on the long road to recovery.

Little by little there were encouraging signs that life was beginning to return to some kind of recognizable form. Members of the royal family continued to drive over to Coppins, and old friends such as Chips Channon, the politician Nancy Astor and Lord ('Bobbety') Cranbourne began paying afternoon visits. Lilia Ralli also proved diverting company, entertaining the royal sisters with amusing stories of times past. By the end of September, Marina felt up to writing replies to some of the messages of sympathy she had received. On the twenty-ninth she picked up one of Cecil Beaton's photographs of George, Michael and herself, to send to President Roosevelt. In her distinguished, slanting caligraphy, on black-edged writing paper embossed with her personal cipher, Marina wrote: 'I want to send you this photograph of your God-son that was taken when he was six weeks old. It is the last one of my husband. I hope I will have the pleasure of introducing him to you in the not too distant future.'

Six weeks later, on 7 November, Queen Wilhelmina of the Netherlands sent Roosevelt her own impressions of Prince Michael. She wrote:

> I had to wait some time after the tragic death of Georgie Kent to go and see our godchild. Now I have just visited Marina and seen little Michael. He is such a darling, and he was in a very good temper, and has such a radiant laugh, and fine big blue eyes and much golden hair, that even stands up in a crest. I think he will later on much resemble his father.

In the event 'little Michael', like his sister Alexandra, grew to resemble Marina. Only Eddie, in almost every single respect, resembled his father. It may be of interest to add at this point that, by succeeding Prince George as the second Duke of Kent, Eddie entered the annals of British royal history, if only as a footnote. At the age of seven he became the youngest prince to succeed to a royal dukedom since 1884, when Queen Victoria's grandson Charles, brother of Princess Alice, Countess of Athlone, was born the second Duke of Albany. His father, Prince Leopold, who had been created the first Duke in 1881, suffered from haemophilia, and it was while on holiday in Cannes with his pregnant wife, Helen of Waldeck-Pyrmont, that he hurt his knee. Next day he died of a brain haemorrhage. When the child Duchess Helen had been carrying was born five months later, he automatically inherited his dead father's title.

Within ten weeks of the Duke of Kent's death Marina put on her Commandant's uniform to fulfil the first public engagement of her widowhood. On 4 November 1942, solemn but composed, she visited a Wren training centre in London. Shortly afterwards it was announced that the Duchess was to assume many of her late husband's patronages, among them those of the Royal School for the Blind at Leatherhead, the Shaftesbury Homes and the training ship *Arethusa*. Later still, in succession to the Duke, Marina was appointed Colonel-in-Chief of the Royal West Kent Regiment (subsequently The Queen's Regiment), from which, on the day of the Duke's funeral, a battalion had been detailed to line the west aisle of St George's Chapel as part of the ceremonial guard-of-honour.

It was to St George's, the magnificent church that Edward iv had commissioned in 1473 and which was finally completed thirty-six years later, that the Duchess of Kent made a poignant visit on 20 December 1942. On what would have been her husband's fortieth birthday, Marina climbed down the dark, narrow staircase, beyond the tombs of Edward vii and Queen Alexandra, to the royal vault, and there laid a wreath of clove carnations on her husband's coffin.

Eleven days later, on New Year's Eve, Princess Olga left England for Kenya, where Prince Paul now lay in a desperate state of ill health. Not long after she had first arrived at Coppins to bring comfort to her sister, Captain Alec Cunningham Reid, Tory MP for St Marylebone, stood up in the House of Commons and, under protection of Parliamentary privilege, fired the first salvo in a slanderous campaign against Princess Olga, that would last for several weeks. Referring to her as a 'sinister woman', and strongly implying that she was a spy, Cunningham Reid finally demanded on 16 December, 'Has not this lady been allowed to be in a position whereby she will be able to convey information to her quisling husband which might be invaluable to the Axis?'

At that, the Foreign Secretary, Anthony Eden, leapt to his feet and sharply rounded on Captain Reid: 'The circumstances are well known. Princess Olga was the only sister of the Duchess of Kent who could come to this country at all and she came here with the Government's authority and approval, and I have no apology to make in the matter.' When Eden had finished speaking, the entire House rang with cheers.

Yet, while the Member for St Marylebone might have been silenced, his tirades had not gone unreported in Kenya, where Prince Paul dared not show his face outside his own front door. Before long, growing ever more depressed by the situation in Yugoslavia, which Germany had ultimately invaded with disastrous consequences; the death of his great friend Prince George; his wife's absence; and Cunningham Reid's bitter invective, the former Prince Regent took to his bed, rarely bothering to get up, refusing all offers of food, and drinking nothing save a daily cup of hot chocolate. Hopes that Princess Olga's return might stem her husband's mental decline were short-lived; so much so, that in February 1943 Prince Paul's doctors feared 'the development of insanity in the form of melancholia'. In London, Churchill continued to resist petitions that Paul and his family be allowed to move to South Africa, but in the end he was brought round. On 11 June Prince and Princess Paul with Alexander, Nicholas and Elisabeth left Kenya for Johannesburg where, free from suspicion and no longer regarded as a prisoner, Paul started to improve.

For Marina, concern over her brother-in-law and the strain his condition imposed on her sister proved curiously therapeutic, helping to direct her thoughts away from her own tragedy. Work also played its part in her recovery and, during 1943, the Duchess of Kent made a permanent return to public life. In addition to the official duties which occupied her time, Marina was to pay tribute to the efforts of her late husband, when she too became a factory inspector. The only difference was that, unlike the Duke, the Duchess fulfilled that function in a purely private, unpublicized capacity. Her success, however, was no less great for that, and in some ways it was an even greater boost to workers' morale. Inexplicably, there was something rather more memorable about meeting an attractive princess than in saying 'How do you do?' to a dozen of the most personable princes.

Another tribute Marina paid to her husband took the traditional royal line of leaving rooms and possessions undisturbed. During November 1942 Chips and Honor Channon spent a weekend at Coppins. Afterwards, Chips noted:

> The Duchess has rearranged her sitting room, kept the
> Duke's just as it was, and has shut up the music room. . . .
> Went up to bed about midnight, and I was haunted by the
> spirit of the Duke. Every room and object is so inspired by
> him, the house, in fact, is him. I met him on the staircase,
> saw him sitting at the end of my bed, as he so often used
> to do, and was constantly aware of him. The house still
> vibrates with his vivacious personality.

Coppins was now officially owned by Eddie. It had been left to him in trust until he came of age. Until he grew up and married, it of course remained very much Marina's home. Indeed, with the exception of a couple of rooms at Marlborough House which Queen Mary put at her disposal, Marina had no other.

When the Kents first moved to Iver, George – like Princess Victoria before him – had soon become a familiar figure in the village and, in time, Marina followed suit. Today local people still remember how walking on a Sunday morning to St Peter's Church – which she entered by a side door, leading to her pew next to the choir – or pottering about the village, the Duchess always 'had a smile and a "good morning" for everyone'.

In a letter to the author, John Evans, who lived in Iver until 1956 and who, as a teenager, was the delivery boy for the local grocers, Platts Stores, provided a brief glimpse into Marina's more domestic existence:

> I used to deliver groceries twice a week to the rear entrance
> of Coppins. I had an errand bike with a huge basket on the
> front. Prince Edward had a ride on it . . . when he was quite

young. The Duchess, wearing an apron and a headscarf, was
often in the kitchen, cooking. A few times on very hot days,
she gave me a home-made ice-cream; a real treat for a wartime lad. She would always call me 'John' and ask about
my family. I suppose even as a boy I was flattered . . . but
that's the kind of person she was. I believe the whole village
loved and respected her. She was a grand lady.

A love of children was one of the most notable features of Princess
Marina's entire life. As a bald statement of fact this may seem,
to some anyway, trite, meaningless and perhaps unnecessary.
Yet given that royal mothers, even in this century, have not always
been capable of establishing a loving relationship with their children – and Queen Mary is probably the safest example to cite
here – Marina proved exceptional. Her love for Eddie, Michael
(or 'Maow', to rhyme with 'now'), and Alexandra ('Pud', short
for 'Pudding', as she became known during her adolescence), was
one of total devotion. Nevertheless as a parent, 'Min', as Marina
was called by her children and other members of the royal
family, tempered indulgence with an insistence on strict discipline, good behaviour and impeccable manners. Even as adults,
Eddie, Pud and Maow ran the risk of incurring their mother's
extreme displeasure by the slightest breach of this rigid code of
conduct.

Another lesson the Duchess instilled into her children was the
value of money. Nothing, she warned, would ever be theirs just
for the asking. One example of this was provided by Clifford
Wade, for many years the chemist in Iver. Eddie and Alexandra
were regular visitors to his shop, and he recalls the occasion when
they came in together to spend the first pocket money they had
ever received. Between them they had exactly sixpence – the equivalent of two and a half pence today – and quite clearly neither
really knew how wisely to spend it or on what. After some time
Mr Wade heard a great deal of conspiratorial whispering and,
looking up, noticed the young Duke and his sister arguing over
a bar of highly perfumed soap. Eddie argued that they would
never be able to use any soap other than that already in the bathrooms at Coppins. Alexandra insisted that they could easily smug-
gle it into the house and nobody need know. She suggested that
she could use it first and then surreptitiously hand it to Eddie

when it was his bathtime. Whether the plan ever worked, only the protagonists themselves could tell. But at all events, in what bordered on triumph, the children handed over their pocket money and gleefully marched from the shop.

To Chips Channon, Princess Alexandra, gauche, gangling and full of energy, was 'a whirlwind of a girl'. Eddie was more diffident, hypersensitive and, on occasion, possessed of much the same bad temper as his father. Michael, on the other hand, while sharing his sister's more even temperament, was as reticent as his brother, perhaps more so. Even as a young man he might ask one of his mother's servants to accompany him to church, lest anybody should recognize him and stop to pass the time of day.

Towards the end of the war, one of Marina's chief considerations was the education of her children. In 1943 Eddie was sent to Ludgrove, a preparatory school near Wokingham in Berkshire. Five years later, as planned at the time of his birth, he went on to Eton. By 1951, however, the Duke had been taken away from England's foremost public school, apparently for reasons of health, and completed his education at Le Rosey in Switzerland. Later he entered the Royal Military Academy at Sandhurst, and was subsequently commissioned into the Royal Scots Dragoon Guards (Carabiniers and Greys).

Like his elder brother, Prince Michael also went to Eton and Sandhurst. After training with the Royal Armoured Corps at Bovington Camp in Dorset, 'Maow' was commissioned into the 11th Hussars, afterwards The Royal Hussars (Prince of Wales's Own).

Academic life for Alexandra was much less rigorous. At the age of eleven she became the first British princess to attend a boarding school. The place chosen by her mother was Heathfield in Ascot, run by Miss Kathleen Dodds, a young and progressive headmistress, who tended to concentrate on the overall development of her students as individuals rather than count the number of potential candidates for university. After Heathfield, Alexandra went to Paris where, during the winter of 1953–54, she stayed with the Comte de Paris and his family, before going on to finishing school. When she returned to London, the Princess took a short nursing course at the Great Ormond Street Hospital for Sick Children.

However and wherever the children were educated, Marina

herself had to foot the bills. Financially, the years from 1943 to 1953 were difficult ones for the Duchess. During her married life, neither she nor her husband had had any money worries whatsoever. Indeed, during 1940, the Duke of Kent had discussed the idea of selling Coppins in order to purchase a much larger property in the Home Counties. Until the start of 1943, Marina's financial status was completely assured. George had money of his own, on top of which he received a more than generous annuity of £25,000 from the Civil List, with substantial periodic increases in prospect during the years ahead. When making his will, therefore, the Duke, a young man in his thirties anticipating a full life, left his personal wealth to his children in trust. When he died, however, his Civil List income died with him. Though scarcely destitute, Marina had not been provided for and, contrary to George's belief, the Civil List at that time did not make provision for royal widows.

As a result Marina's only recourse, no matter how 'humiliating', as she put it, was to sell some of George's possessions in order to boost her capital and maintain a standard of living at least similar to the one she had been used to. The first sale, in November 1943, consisted of furniture left to Prince George in 1939 by his great-aunt Princess Louise, Duchess of Argyll. George himself had already decided to sell the furniture since he didn't want it, and at auction it fetched almost £20,000. Four years later, in March 1947, a further £92,341 was raised when the Duchess sent a quantity of furniture, pictures, silver and porcelain to be auctioned at Christie's.

To help out, both George VI and Queen Mary provided Marina with private – and therefore undisclosed – allowances, and in that way she managed to exist on a comfortable basis until the early 1950s. Then, despite the fact that it did not constitute the full, official annuity she had hoped to receive as one of the most active members of the royal family, Elizabeth II allocated her aunt a sum estimated at £5,000 a year, out of an extra £25,000 voted by Parliament when the Civil List came under review at the start of the new reign.

It is undeniably true that, as a widow, the Duchess – who left only £54,121 net when she died – was never as excessively rich as some of her royal in-laws. None the less, repeated claims, which are still heard today, that she was 'poverty-stricken' are patently absurd. Poverty is, of course, a relative condition, but strictly defined it means hardship and deprivation or, to quote from the dictionary, 'not having the means to procure comforts or necessaries of life'. It is difficult to believe that such a definition ever applied to the Duchess of Kent.

Consider, for example, that when Marina was allocated a grace-and-favour residence at Kensington Palace, she employed a permanent staff of eleven. Excluding a full-time private secretary and office personnel, Min's household consisted of a butler, housekeeper, three footmen, two housemaids, a chef, a switchboard operator – manning six lines and thirty extensions – and two chauffeurs. Until the mid-1960s, when it was sold in favour of a later and slightly larger, black model, the Duchess travelled everywhere by road in a deep-blue Rolls-Royce, registration YR II. (This personal number plate, originally adopted by Prince George when he and his brother David lived together at York House, is said to read 'York Royal Two'.)

It should also be considered that, throughout the twenty-six years of her widowhood, whether in the beautiful salons at Coppins or Kensington Palace, Marina continued to entertain in a style Prince George would certainly have recognized as his own. She continued to make frequent private trips abroad; and as for clothes, though thorough in her costings, which were always made in advance of any firm orders, Marina's wardrobe continued to be replenished with couture outfits by designers such as John Cavanagh, Norman Hartnell and Victor Stiebel. At her death Marina bequeathed a spectacular collection of jewellery to her daughter and daughter-in-law, with an extra provision for the wife Prince Michael would undoubtedly take at some future time.

While it is obvious that Princess Marina's wealth could not be estimated – at least in its entirety – in terms of liquid assets, the comfort in which she lived and the style to which she had been accustomed since the time of her marriage suggest that she was not the penurious widow of popular legend.

Throughout the Second World War the Duchess of Kent's first cousin, Prince Philip of Greece and Denmark, only son of her father's brother, Prince Andrew, served in the British Royal Navy.

Having already proved himself an outstanding cadet at Dartmouth, where he won the coveted King's Dirk, Philip went on to prove himself a worthy and astute officer in action. Aboard HMS *Valiant*, during the battle of Cape Matapan, 'his alertness and appreciation of the situation', as his commanding officer reported in dispatches, 'resulted in the sinking of two eight-inch gun Italian cruisers' in the space of five minutes.

When not at sea the tall, Nordic-looking prince was frequently to be found at Coppins. And when Philip was there the King's elder daughter, Princess Elizabeth – known as 'Lilibet' – was rarely very far away. Marina, who in 1944 had done much to further the romance between another of her cousins, Alexandra of Greece and the exiled King Peter of Yugoslavia, for whom her brother-in-law Prince Paul had acted as regent, derived great pleasure at watching an even more significant courtship develop under her own roof.

For some considerable time Philip and Lilibet had waited for the King to give his consent to their engagement, and in July 1947 George VI finally gave in. At the couple's wedding in Westminster Abbey four months later, on 20 November, the eleven-year-old Princess Alexandra was to act as one of her cousin's eight bridesmaids; while five-year-old Prince Michael and six-year-old Prince William of Gloucester (who would also lose his life in an air crash) were to be Princess Elizabeth's train-bearers. At the wedding rehearsal in the Abbey, as Sir Michael Duff related to Cecil Beaton afterwards, 'Michael of Kent punched cousin William of Gloucester in the kisser . . . which alarmed our Duchess [Marina] considerably, and he received a good talking to from Granny, who with parasol in hand, was prepared for action should it occur again on THE DAY.'

On THE DAY, the bride's bouquet went missing and the band of her tiara snapped in two, causing panic at the palace; but at Westminster Abbey the two pageboys behaved themselves with the utmost restraint and decorum. At this – the last truly royal wedding Britain might ever see, inasmuch as both bride and bridegroom were born Royal Highnesses – Alexandra, in her star-spangled ivory tulle dress, also passed the ordeal with flying colours. A day or two later, however, when she was back at school, she begged not to have to join a party of Heathfield girls on an outing to a local cinema. On offer was a film of the royal wedding, and the young princess had no wish to see herself on the wide screen. If made to go, she remonstrated, she would surely die of embarrassment.

For the Duchess of Kent, the 1940s ended on a far happier note than they had begun. The war was over; she had come to terms with the loss of her husband; her home life, in spite of its inevitable changes, followed a basically happy and comfortable pattern; her mother and sisters were again free; and, as always, she was surrounded by friends who adored her. In 1948 Marina, who even during the war had featured regularly in the pages of newspapers drastically reduced in size and content, was as newsworthy as ever, cropping up at a variety of daytime events, gala functions, dinner parties and soirées in a way that was reminiscent of the days when she and George dazzled London and, with the Prince of Wales, dominated the social scene of the 1930s. At the start of the year, for instance, the diary pages noted that the Duchess had attended a service at St Mark's Church, North Audley Street, in Mayfair, in remembrance of Mrs Laura Corrigan, American-born multi-millionairess, society hostess and one-time telephonist from Cleveland, Ohio. For the late Mrs Corrigan, rival of such famous hostesses as Lady Cunard and Mrs Ronnie Greville, it was exactly the kind of tribute she would have revelled in; especially since the Duchess of Kent had never attended a non-royal memorial service before.

A little later, on 17 February, at a party given by Mrs Sacheverell Sitwell for Mae West, who was then appearing in *Diamond Lil* at the Prince of Wales's Theatre, Marina not only met the legendary star herself but also the American comedian and movie actor Danny Kaye. On 1 March their paths crossed yet again. That evening Chips Channon, inveterate collector of crowned heads, princelings and celebrities, gave an 'immense supper party' at his house in Belgrave Square, in honour of the 'mesmeric' Mr Kaye, who was currently starring in his own show at the London Palladium. For Marina and the celebrated entertainer, it was the start of a very special but little discussed relationship.

Chapter Fifteen

The Duchess Regrets

Within the Duchess of Kent's private coterie, Lady Zia Wernher (formerly Countess Anastasia de Torby, daughter of the Grand Duke Michael of Russia); the squeaky-voiced Lilia Ralli (nicknamed 'Figgi', because of her constant use of the expression '*figure-toi*', which roughly translated means 'you know'); Turia Campbell (born a Princess Galitzine); Zoia Poklewska-Koziell and her mother Baroness Agnes de Stoeckl (to whom Marina leased a cottage on the Coppins estate) were among her closest women friends. Though not all were able to claim imperial descent, they nevertheless formed a kind of bridge which linked the nostalgic past with the more prosaic, egalitarian present.

Often they would gather round Marina's dining table, chattering, joking, exchanging the latest news of friends and relations scattered around the world. Although the Duchess herself abhorred and would never listen to gossip, particularly of a malicious or unkind nature, she always regarded these conversations among trusted friends as strictly private. Indeed, the very moment the butler or a footman entered the room, Marina would stop speaking in English and, without a flicker of hesitation, switch to one of several languages common to her circle. Even between Marina and her sisters there was a language – perhaps a mixture of Russian and Greek – few admit to ever having understood.

Through their professions other, predominantly male, friends – such as Noël Coward, Danny Kaye, Douglas Fairbanks and Cecil Beaton – transported the Duchess to another world – the world of entertainment. After the war Noël Coward became a regular escort, though theirs was not a friendship Queen Mary ever viewed with favour. Many times she wrote to her son's widow, indicating that she should terminate her relationship with a man who, in the Dowager's opinion, was not quite the ticket. Marina's stout response was to ignore Queen Mary's letters.

As with the diaries Coward kept during the 1930s and '40s, so his journals for the '50s and '60s were liberally sprinkled with references to Princess Marina. On 25 June 1951, for instance, he wrote, 'Went with the Duchess of Kent to Covent Garden to hear *Bohème* – Victoria de los Angeles sang well but looked like a musical bun .... Took the Duchess to dine at the Ivy, and then on to the Palladium for the Sid Field Benefit .... Highest spot – Judy Garland.' As the years passed there were many such references, some more fleeting than others: 'Lunched with the Duchess and Princess Alexandra', 'had tea with Princess Marina', and so on. Despite Queen Mary's disapproval Coward was a genuine friend who adored being with the Duchess, whether entertaining her in lavish style or merely dropping in for a quiet chat over a drink or two.

Beyond the company Marina kept in private, lay the inescapable and often much less glamorous responsibilities of her public role. To many the Princess's name was immediately synonymous with the world-famous tennis championships at Wimbledon, which she attended without fail every summer, and with her presidency of the celebrated charity founded by her great-aunt Queen Alexandra.

It was during the 1950s, when Marina made one of her annual tours of Alexandra Rose Day fairs and depots in London, that she was attended by Lady Constance Milnes-Gaskell. Once a lady-in-waiting to Queen Mary, Lady Constance had always been used to walking round the back of a royal car to get in by the off-side door – it was evidently never done to climb across the old Queen Dowager herself. On this particular occasion Princess Marina had taken leave of her hosts at the Park Lane Hotel in Piccadilly and had settled herself in the back of her Rolls-Royce. As the car moved off, the Princess leaned forward and asked her chauffeur, Albert Jones, 'Are we not taking Lady Constance with us on the rest of the tour?' Immediately glancing into his rear-view mirror, the avuncular Mr Jones was horrified to see the helpless lady-in-waiting still standing in the middle of the road. Not without some embarrassment, he slowly reversed the car to collect the speechless attendant. Highly amused though she was, Marina reproached Lady

Constance, 'You're not with Queen Mary now. You know, you really must remember to get in the same side as I do.'

Though she undertook endless official engagements in her own right, the Duchess of Kent frequently appeared in public with other members of the royal family. She invariably joined them to witness the annual ceremony of Trooping the Colour on Horse Guards Parade, attended the State Opening of Parliament, a genuinely feudal ritual enacted with great solemnity in the House of Lords, and took part in ceremonial occasions such as state visits by foreign heads of state. Between the spring of 1950 and the early summer of 1951, for example, there were four such visits, made by President Auriol of France, Queen Juliana of the Netherlands, King Frederick of Denmark and King Haakon of Norway.

Each June, then as now, there were also the races at Ascot, when society invaded the quiet Berkshire backwater as much to be seen in their smartest fashions as to back some hotly-tipped filly in the 3.30. To the traditionally minded the highlight of each of the four days covered by the meeting is inevitably the arrival of the royal family. Leaving Windsor Castle shortly after lunchtime, the royal party makes its way in a convoy of gleaming Rolls-Royce limousines up to Duke's Meadow in Windsor Great Park. There cars are swapped for carriages – small postilion landaus with basket-weave sides – preceded by out-riders in scarlet coats and black top hats. The royal procession drives through the Park to Watersplash Lane and Cheapside in neighbouring Sunninghill, thence to Ascot race-course itself.

Once there the carriages pass through the famous Golden Gates to drive down the entire length of the course to the royal enclosure. Once infinitely more elitist than it is today, Royal Ascot has enjoyed the patronage of the rich, the famous and, of course, the royal, ever since Queen Anne inaugurated the races on Ascot Heath in August 1711.

By the summer of 1952 the face of Britain's monarchy had changed. The King was dead and the 'Age of the New Elizabethans', as the media were calling the reign of his daughter Elizabeth II, had been ushered in against a background of private tears and public fanfares. It was, therefore, as the representative of a new sovereign and a new era that the Duchess of Kent undertook her first official overseas tour. Inspiration for the five-week visit to Singapore, Malaya, Sarawak, North Borneo and Hong Kong had sprung from an invitation made to the Duchess on behalf of the Singapore Anti-Tuberculosis Association to open their new clinic. As President of the National Association for the Prevention of Tuberculosis in England, Marina had no hesitation in accepting. It was then suggested that while in Singapore the Duchess, as Commandant, might visit the Women's Royal Naval Service and, as Colonel-in-Chief, fly to Kuala Lumpur in Malaya, to inspect the 1st Battalion, The Queen's Own Royal West Kent Regiment, at their headquarters at Kuala Kubu Bahru.

Once the framework of the visit had been properly established, a further sixty-five official engagements were organized and slotted into the Duchess's provisional schedule. Within three months her every move had been plotted and timed to run like clockwork. On Saturday 27 September 1952, accompanied by her son Eddie, Marina left London aboard the BOAC Argonaut aircraft *Atalanta*, in which the then Princess Elizabeth had flown to Kenya eight months earlier.

With the Duchess and the sixteen-year-old Duke of Kent travelled Lady Rachel Davidson, sister of Bernard, Duke of Norfolk, the Earl Marshal. Also in the party was Viscount Althorp, temporarily seconded to the Duchess's party. 'Johnnie' Althorp, then twenty-eight, had been equerry to George VI and was briefly equerry to Elizabeth II. Today he is better known as the Eighth Earl Spencer, father of Diana, Princess of Wales.

Another member of the Duchess of Kent's entourage was the swarthy Philip Hay who, at thirty-four, had been Marina's private secretary since 1948, the year in which he married Lady Margaret Seymour, then a lady-in-waiting to Princess Elizabeth. By no means all who serve members of the royal family in the capacity of private secretary are schooled in charm, and the abrasive Philip Hay was living evidence of that fact. Eventually, as seems to happen automatically with untitled private secretaries, Hay was knighted; though not, as many who had dealings with him agreed, for his contribution to the diplomatic art of public relations. When receiving visitors who, in one way or another, did business with his royal mistress, for example, Hay would all too frequently follow a formal welcome with a terse 'I suppose you know why you are here?' There were, in fact, several occasions when the visitor, having turned up only because he had been summoned, actually did not have a clue. But such was the brusque exterior of the man who was to serve Princess Marina for twenty years and whose support ultimately transcended the boundaries separating professional obligation from a more intimate relationship. Indeed, Hay came to represent something of a father-figure to the Duchess's children; especially to the youngest, Prince Michael, whose interests he continued to manage long after Marina died.

On that September day in 1952 the Duchess of Kent's party left Heathrow Airport to fly south and east to Rome, Cyprus, and Bahrain, where they spent a few hours as the guests of Sheik Sulman bin Hamed al-Khalifah at his palace in Manama. Then they flew on to Ceylon, now Sri Lanka, where the Duchess and her son were welcomed by the Prime Minister, Dudley Senanayake, at the start of a twenty-four-hour visit to Colombo. The following day, as the royal aircraft approached Singapore, six Vampire jet fighters flew out to escort it to Kallang Airport where, to the thud of a 21-gun salute, the *Atalanta* taxied to a halt in front of the guard of honour. There among assorted dignitaries waiting to greet Marina and Eddie were John Fearns Nicoll, the Governor of Singapore, and Malcolm MacDonald, Commissioner-General for the United Kingdom in South-East Asia. From the airport, the royal cavalcade drove past thousands of flag-waving children towards Government House. Set in a magnificent tropical garden and resembling something that might have been erected somewhere in India during the days of the Raj, the mansion had been built in 1865 and once accommodated Queen Victoria's son 'Affie', Duke of Edinburgh, during an Empire tour in 1869. From Government House the Duchess of Kent visited the Royal Naval base, the Admiralty Asian School, the University of Singapore, the 4th Independent Company of the Women's Royal Army Corps and the British Military Hospital – and, of course, opened the anti-tuberculosis clinic that had originally sparked off the idea of the Duchess's tour.

On 5 October the royal visitors flew to Malaya, then still rife with jungle warfare. On her way to the headquarters of the West Kent Regiment, in a tiny village forty miles from Kuala Lumpur, the Duchess drove through terrain notorious for terrorist activity. In fact, on the day of the visit itself the Suffolk Regiment had shot and killed one terrorist, while troops and police had discovered slit trenches for fifty men overlooking the road, from which it became clear that the royal party were meant to have been ambushed. It was said that the would-be assassins had fled not more than three days earlier, after RAF strafing and regular security patrols.

By comparison, Marina's visits to Sarawak and North Borneo were sedate affairs, though she did receive a deputation of Malay, Dyak, Melanaus, Kayan, Kenyah and Murut tribesmen, who had only recently given up head-hunting. As proof of his former occupation one Dyak headsman proudly showed the Duchess a lock of hair he wore in his sword belt, telling her that it had come from the severed head of a Japanese officer unlucky enough to have crossed the tribe's path. In North Borneo the Duchess opened Marina Barracks, the new police headquarters, and the recently completed Duchess of Kent Hospital. The tour continued with a visit to Brunei where, upon her arrival, Marina was carried to the Sultan's palace in a state litter. Once there, according to custom, she was conducted to a canopied daïs from where she listened to a speech of welcome read by the bespectacled Sultan, Omar Ali Saifuddin, himself. At the oil town of Seria, the Duchess was invited to christen a new oil well named after her, which in traditional style she did, carefully aiming a bottle of champagne at the narrow drilling bit. After Brunei came a five-day visit to Hong Kong, before the official visitors returned briefly to Singapore. When the Duchess flew home to England, arriving on 2 December, she and Eddie were met at Heathrow by a full reception committee – the Queen and the Duke of Edinburgh, the Queen Mother, Princess Margaret, the Duchess of Gloucester, Princess Alexandra and Prince Michael.

Later that month, the Duchess of Kent and her three children journeyed up to Norfolk to spend Christmas with the rest of the royal family at Sandringham. After the Duke died, Marina seldom made holiday visits to Scotland – where she and George had always occupied Birkhall on the Balmoral estate – but she did make a point of joining her husband's family at Sandringham each December.

Christmas 1952 was not without its sadder aspects, especially for Marina's sister-in-law Queen Elizabeth. For the first time in twenty-nine years she found herself without the King and in the very house in which he had died only ten months before. Some time later the Queen Mother commiserated with a recently widowed friend, when she wrote: 'I do hope Christmas time did not make you feel too sad. It is such a thing of memories I find, and one is thankful when it is over. . . .'

By the time the royal family reassembled at Sandringham for the Christmas holiday of 1953 three more of its members would be absent. Marina's mother-in-law Queen Mary had died in London on 24 March at the age of eighty-five, and the Queen and the Duke of Edinburgh were in New Zealand on the first phase of their six-month coronation tour of the Commonwealth.

Of the immediate members of her own family, Marina was now the only one caught up in the public round of royal duties. To all intents and purposes, Princess Nicholas at home in Athens, Elizabeth in her castle in Bavaria, and Olga, now living in Paris, were all private citizens. Long since freed from royal obligations of any kind, Olga and Paul were able to travel more or less wherever and whenever they pleased. They would have liked to settle permanently in Britain, but public opinion was such that only a fool would have seriously contemplated such a move.

The royal family and Paul's genuine friends in England were as happy to see him as they had always been. Otherwise the stigma of treason that he would nearly always wear when in Britain meant that he was an unwelcome visitor to these shores. As a visitor he came just the same, though in 1954 his presence was touched by tragedy. Five years earlier Paul and Olga's younger son Nicholas had followed in his father's footsteps to Christ Church, Oxford, then in 1952 had joined a city banking firm. On the night of 12 April 1954 the twenty-five-year-old prince, who had been to a party near Windsor, was heading back to London through Datchet, when his sports car skidded, overturned, and threw Nicholas face down into a ditch. He drowned in a few inches of water. At Coppins, where the family assembled, Marina tried to comfort her sister and brother-in-law in their tremendous grief. Nicholas's funeral took place at the Church of St Peter in Iver a few days later. There, throughout the night before the funeral, Paul sat alone by his son's coffin. Outside two local policemen stood guard by the door, a deterrent to reporters and any other unwelcome visitors. Nicholas of Yugoslavia lies buried immediately behind the church – though, to judge from its appearance in the summer of 1987, the grave, hidden by tall grass and covered with debris from surrounding trees, has seen few visitors in the intervening years.

Sharing the agony of Paul and Olga's bereavement was a painful reminder of all the hours Marina herself had sat in the silent rooms at Coppins, mourning the death of Prince George not quite twelve years before. By the spring of 1954, however, the Duchess had accepted the tenancy of a grace-and-favour apartment at Kensington Palace, which meant that Coppins would now see rather less of Marina and her family.

The house she had been offered occupies much of the south wing of the red-brick palace Wren had built for William and Mary during the late seventeenth century. Beyond the imposing porte-cochère with its pillars and crown-topped lanterns, through the King's Gallery, to the first of the state apartments, the four-storey house originally contained some forty rooms. It looks across Kensington Gardens in one direction; across the old parade ground, now a grassy enclosure, in another; and directly into the private quadrangle known as Clock Court on the far side. After William and Mary and their successors, Queen Anne and the Prince of Denmark, the house was lived in by the first two Georges. They were followed by the controversial Caroline of Brunswick, estranged wife of the Prince Regent, afterwards George IV. Later still, the Regent's brother, Augustus, Duke of Sussex, occupied the house where, on the first floor, he established the famous Sussex Library. The last occupants were Queen Victoria's daughter Princess Louise – an accomplished painter and sculptress – and her husband, John Campbell, Marquess of Lorne, afterwards ninth Duke of Argyll. Despite the fact that the Argylls' marriage was never a happy one, the house was to be Louise's home from the time of her marriage in 1871 until her death in 1939.

It was in that year that King George VI promised the apartment to the Duke and Duchess of Kent. The intervention of the war naturally meant that any plans George and Marina might have had for making Kensington Palace their London base had to be shelved indefinitely. Now, some fifteen years later, Elizabeth II repeated her father's offer. Happy though the Duchess was to accept, she explained that, in its entirety, the house would be far too big for her family's needs. By way of compromise, it was agreed to convert the property into two separate residences: Apartments 1 and 1A.

In 1954 the cost of the conversion, together with desperately needed interior renovation, was estimated at £80,000. In the event, it cost £127,000 and furious MPs demanded to know why, 'having regard to the urgent need for economy', the Government was prepared to foot the bill at that juncture. Marina was deeply upset at the furore from both Conservatives and Socialists, given that the work was vital if the palace, as part of the national heritage, was to be made secure and habitable. Seven years later much the same argument was raised in Parliament when Princess Margaret and Lord Snowdon were allocated £55,000 for the restoration of Apartment 1A. There was, of course, every justification for asking why, after years of rationing and austerity, hard-pressed taxpayers, who already handsomely subsidized the monarchy, should be expected to provide one forty-seven-year-old war widow with a second home. After all, were there not still thousands of war widows with no real homes at all?

Despite the protests, work on Apartment 1 went ahead and, on 21 October 1955, the Duchess of Kent finally moved in. For the eight years of her marriage, Marina had deferred to the personal likes and dislikes of her husband. Since his death she had become as assertive as she had been for the first twenty-seven years of her life. Now at Kensington Palace that assertiveness, which George had once put down to bossiness, was required to make the kinds of household decisions that had formerly been exclusively his.

In some respects the home Marina created at Apartment 1 reflected George's influence, but essentially it bore *her* stamp. At the end of a long gallery – which in turn led from the main entrance hall, where the Duchess always kept fresh arrangements of yellow and white flowers – lay a kind of inner-hall where Marina hung de Laszlo's portrait of Princess Nicholas. Off to the right was a comfortable sitting room, from which french doors led down into a secluded walled garden. Beyond the staircase to the left of the inner hallway lay the office Marina shared with Philip Hay, while next door was a large and rather splendid drawing room, with eighteenth-century furniture, fine pictures, country-house chintzes and a wealth of exquisite *objets d'art*, including pieces by Carl Fabergé, court jeweller to the Tsars of Russia. On the second floor were the family's bedrooms, dressing rooms, and guest rooms; while below in the basement were to be found the household offices.

Before the Snowdons moved into Apartment 1A in 1962, and long before Kensington Palace became the royal commune it is today, Marina's nearest royal neighbour was Princess Alice, Countess of Athlone. She and Aunt Alice both attended the same church, St Mary Abbots, no more than a five-minute walk from the palace itself. In fact, since Princess Alice did not possess a car of her own, she would travel about London by bus or, as she preferred, on foot. On one occasion as Marina was driving back from an official engagement, she spotted the elderly Princess trotting up Sloane Street. Instructing her chauffeur to pull over, the Duchess asked if she would like a lift back home. Queen Victoria's granddaughter looked up at the sky and shook her head. 'It's not going to rain, Min,' she said, 'I think I'll walk.'

Had Marina ever wanted to remarry, Kensington Palace might not have been her home for very long. Indeed, had she accepted one proposal during the spring of 1957, she would have left England permanently to become Crown Princess – and very soon Queen – of Norway. At that time Crown Prince Olav, the present King Olav v, had been a widower for three years. Married in 1929, he had lost his wife Märtha, daughter of the Swedish Duke of Västergotland, in April 1954, since when he had been urged to marry again. Various princesses had been suggested, but the Crown Prince was interested only in Marina of Kent.

By virtue of his parentage – his mother, Queen Maud, was the youngest of Edward vii's three daughters; his Danish-born father, King Haakon vii, was the second son of King Frederick viii of Denmark – Olav was extremely close to both the British and Danish royal families. It was therefore to his Danish cousin Rico (King Frederick ix) that Olav turned in order to ask a special favour. Notwithstanding the delicate irony of the situation, for it will be remembered that the King of Denmark had once been engaged to the Duchess of Kent's sister Olga, Rico agreed to act as the Norwegian Prince's special envoy. In a manner recalling the diplomatic preliminaries to arranged marriages of centuries past, Rico flew to London. Over lunch at Clarence House, he explained the nature of his visit to the Queen Mother and recruited her to act as go-between. A few days later, 'the tea-cosy', as Marina and her family called Queen Elizabeth, invited her sister-in-law to lunch. It was then that Marina learnt of Olav's proposal. Charmed though she was, the Duchess nevertheless declined.

Interestingly enough, stories that Marina and Olav were to marry had first appeared in the press three years earlier. At about the same time, another alleged suitor was Sir Anthony Eden. Yet perhaps one of the most curious rumours of all had first appeared in October 1945, when the Belgian newspaper *Libre Belgique* claimed that Marina was to marry their very own Regent, the forty-one-year-old Prince Charles. It was, of course, nothing more than idle speculation, but for some reason the Belgian press seemed anxious to marry the Regent off to a member of the British royal family. After the Duchess of Kent, who was at least of the same generation, the Belgians decided that Charles was now about to become engaged to Princess Elizabeth, George VI's twenty-year-old daughter.

Marina's decision not to remarry was clearly her way of paying tribute both to Prince George and to their children. Yet even so, as a comparatively young widow – she was barely thirty-nine at the war's end – she neither disguised nor denied the need for romance in her life. From the time she married, Marina was famous for exercising discretion in all things. Never was that fact illustrated to better advantage than in the affairs she had with men of prominence, notably from the spheres of politics and show business. Of them all, however, perhaps *the* love story of Marina's widowhood was her relationship with Danny Kaye. Whenever he visited Britain, he always made straight for Kensington Palace or Coppins. It was, of course, because he blended so naturally into Marina's celebrated circle that few outsiders ever suspected that he and the Duchess were more than just good friends.

Chapter Sixteen

An Untroubled End

By the close of the 1950s Eddie Kent had met Katharine Worsley, the young Yorkshirewoman he wanted to marry. In the course of her social whirl, Alexandra – who at one time hoped to wed the Irish peer Raymond O'Neill, stepson of Ian Fleming – had also met her future husband, the Honourable Angus Ogilvy.

Marina's attitude to the more personal aspects of her son and daughter's lives was ambivalent. The moment Eddie married, she would cease to be *the* Duchess of Kent – a thought which certainly did not please her – and though she rather coveted one or two of Alexandra's beaux, personable young men with aristocratic backgrounds, in her eyes none was entirely right for her daughter. Like most mothers, Marina wanted the best for her children and, when it came to matrimony, the best meant only one thing – *royalty*. With Eddie in mind, the Duchess might have named any one of several eligible princesses; Margrethe and Benedikte, daughters of Rico and Ingrid of Denmark, for instance, or Beatrix and Irene, elder daughters of Juliana and Bernhard of the Netherlands. The possibilities for a dynastic alliance were almost limitless; for a royal marriage, born of love, they were not. For Alexandra, there was only one decent catch: Harald of Norway. Educated at Balliol College, Oxford, he was the only son of Marina's one-time suitor King Olav. It was well known in royal circles that the Duchess of Kent would like to have seen her daughter become Crown Princess – and eventually Queen – of that Scandinavian kingdom.

In affairs of the heart, relatively few mothers give unconditional approval to their offsprings' choice of partner, and Marina was no exception. Between a mother and her sons there also exists that peculiarly indefinable bond which so often causes friction when daughters-in-law take their rightful place within a family. As a person, Marina entirely approved of the delightful Miss Worsley; but Kate, as she was known, was not a princess, nor did she have a title, and there was no real money of which to speak. Kate was also nearly three years older than Eddie who, though in his early twenties, was not the most extrovert of men and was scarcely a budding Lothario. Was Eddie too young? Was Kate a little too old? Were they really right for each other? Through uncertainty, Marina prevaricated, deliberately withholding consent to her son's marriage for almost three years. Eddie went away to Germany with his regiment, and Katharine went to Canada to stay with one of her brothers and his family. When they returned home a year later, their feelings for one another had withstood the test, and the Duchess finally gave them her blessing.

On 8 March 1961 the engagement of Edward, Duke of Kent, and Katharine, only daughter of Sir William and Lady Worsley of Hovingham, was formally announced in the Court Circular. The wedding itself was arranged for Thursday 8 June. But instead of taking place at Westminster Abbey, the 'union' to which the Queen had 'gladly given her consent' was to be celebrated at York Minster, twenty miles or so from the Worsley family's home at Hovingham Hall.

Three weeks before the wedding, amid all the hustle and bustle of final preparations, Marina flew up to Scotland to inspect the Wrens at Lossiemouth on the Moray Firth. Forty miles away across the water, between the villages of Dunbeath and Berriedale, lay the site of the Sunderland flying boat disaster. On 16 May, Eddie and Alexandra joined Marina at the end of her visit to Lossiemouth, and together they made a pilgrimage to the five-foot Celtic cross which serves as a memorial to Prince George, Frank Goyen, John Lowther, and the rest of the men who died with them at that remote spot on 25 August 1942. It was perhaps the family's way of letting George know that he had not been forgotten at a time of family celebration.

In York on 8 June the entire British royal family, accompanied by a host of foreign royal relations, made their way from the railway station to the Cathedral Church of St Peter, as the Minster is properly known. Among the guests was Queen Victoria Eugenie of Spain, the British princess who had married King Alfonso XIII in May 1906. Daughter of Beatrice, Princess Henry of Battenberg (Queen Victoria's youngest child), 'Ena' had had her wedding day spoilt when an anarchist's bomb exploded next to the bridal carriage, showering the new Queen with broken glass and spattering her wedding gown with blood from some of the men and horses that had been part of the ceremonial escort.

Seated behind 'Cousin Ena' at York, more than fifty years later, was her grandson the Infante Juan Carlos, Prince of the Asturias, now King Juan Carlos of Spain. Two places away sat Princess Sofia of the Hellenes, elder daughter of Marina's cousin King Paul. Neither Juan Carlos nor Sofia had met before, but their introduction that day led to their own wedding in Athens two years later on 14 May 1962.

Next to Marina, stunningly dressed in champagne-coloured organdie, and Alexandra in azalea pink, sat Paul and Olga. A few years earlier, the family party would have been completed by their mother and middle sister, Elizabeth. Now both were dead. Princess Nicholas had died of a heart attack in 1957; Elizabeth in 1955.

At the reception held afterwards at Hovingham Hall, Cecil Beaton photographed the bridal couple in all their wedding finery; Eddie in the ceremonial uniform of the Royal Scots Greys; Katharine, the new Duchess of Kent, in a diaphanous gown of white silk gauze, with the narrow diamond tiara Marina had given to her securing her silk tulle veil. Hugo Vickers tells us that Beaton was taking

> 'the only good picture of the day, one of the bride alone'
> when Richard Colville, the officious press secretary, shouted
> at Cecil to do as he was told and take groups. This prevented
> Cecil from providing the bridal pair with anything more of
> interest, the sad result of a misguided devotion to duty.
> Having taken the groups, Cecil enjoyed the passing show,
> especially when Princess Marina and the Duke of Kent
> handed their cigarettes to Sir Philip Hay 'who became a
> mobile human ashtray'.

Of the twenty-eight-year-old Duchess, Beaton later wrote that she was 'a very nice ordinary girl, with an unusual strength of character'. In time Katharine, an attractive, well-spoken blonde, revealed herself to be not only a more than worthy successor to her mother-in-law, but the most gracious addition to the royal family since Marina herself. During the 1980s, through her private and largely unpublicized work for the Helen House children's hospice, the Samaritans and Age Concern, the Duchess would also reveal characteristics of tenderness and compassion which earned her both the nation's praise and its admiration.

With her son's marriage, Marina chose to be known officially as Princess Marina, Duchess of Kent, rather than use the equally correct, but more outmoded title Dowager Duchess of Kent. It was then that Apartment 1 at Kensington Palace became her only residence. Among those who knew Marina well some maintain that she felt bitter about the loss of her title, as well as the loss of Coppins, the house she and George had moved into a quarter of a century before. If that is true, she also bowed to the inevitable with equanimity.

After a leisurely honeymoon spent partly at Birkhall on the Balmoral estate, and partly in Spain, Eddie and Katharine flew out to Hong Kong, where the Duke was serving with his regiment. It was from there, towards the end of the year, that Marina learned she was soon to become a grandmother. Some six months later, on 26 June 1962, the Kents' first child, the Earl of St Andrews was born at Coppins and given the name of George in honour of his dead grandfather. Another family celebration that year took place only five months later when, on 29 November, a day which would have been George and Marina's twenty-eighth wedding anniversary, Princess Alexandra's engagement to the Honourable Angus Ogilvy was announced. Second son of the Twelfth Earl of Airlie, Angus was also the grandson of Mabell, Countess of Airlie, to whom long ago, when he was fighting a battle of wits with his father, Prince George had confided his wish to leave the Navy and join the Civil Service.

Alexandra and Angus – at that time a city businessman with no fewer than fifty-six directorships to his credit – were married at Westminster Abbey on 24 April 1963. Now only the twenty-one-year-old Prince Michael was left at home. The wedding of Princess Alexandra had given rise to much excitement; but royal weddings are over as quickly as anyone else's and, within the space of twenty-four hours, it had become just one more event to be indexed and stored away in newspaper archives. The year 1963, however, lingered on in the public's memory not so much as the year of the royal wedding, but as the year in which one of the most publicized court cases this century was brought to the Old Bailey.

The protagonists in the drama were Dr Stephen Ward, a well-known society osteopath and artist; John Profumo, MP, Minister of War in the Government of Harold Macmillan, and two callgirls, Christine Keeler and Mandy Rice-Davies – chief witnesses for the prosecution. In their book *An Affair of State*, Philip Knightley and Caroline Kennedy remind us that

> Stephen Ward [whom Lord Denning, Master of the Rolls, described as the 'most evil man' he had ever met] was a central figure in the political scandal which shook Britain. It was in Ward's flat that John Profumo . . . used to meet . . . Christine Keeler. It was Ward who introduced Christine to the dashing Soviet diplomat, Yevgeny Ivanov. It was Ward who told MI5 about Profumo because he thought that their affair might pose a security risk. When Profumo lied to the House of Commons about his love life, and the resulting scandal threatened to bring down the Government, it was Ward who stood in the dock . . . scapegoat for the establishment.

For two months society talked of little else. Among those who had met Stephen Ward and followed the case with avidity were several members of the royal family. Princess Marina was one who had encountered Ward as he breezed through the lives of the rich and famous and, like Prince Philip, Princess Margaret, the Duke and Duchess of Gloucester, and Eddie and Katharine, Marina had sat for him at Kensington Palace. Ward said afterwards that hers was the most difficult likeness to capture: 'The mouth is ever so slightly askew, the sort of thing in a drawing that is extremely hard not to overdo. The result didn't please me and I don't think it pleased her.'

What pleased Marina even less was seeing John Profumo, who had been a friend for some while, feature so very prominently in the whole squalid and humiliating business. That June Profumo had resigned both as Minister of War and as an MP, but Marina, unlike some, did not turn her back on the disgraced minister or his wife Valerie. Scandal had never touched Marina's life, but – if only by implication – it might easily have done so during the summer of 1963. Even so, there was only one occasion on which she failed to keep an engagement with the Profumos. On 3 August, as the case at the Old Bailey was about to be wrapped up and sentence passed, John and Valerie were to have dined with the Princess at Kensington Palace. That day, however, Stephen Ward, who had 'swallowed enough Nembutal tablets to kill a horse', died in St Stephen's Hospital, Fulham. When the news was announced, Princess Marina cancelled her dinner party and, perhaps feeling the need to breathe some fresher air, decided to leave London to spend a few days in Scotland.

For Princess Marina, as for the rest of the royal family, the following spring was made especially memorable by the fact that she and the Queen Mother were each presented with a brace of grandchildren apiece. On Leap Year's day Princess Alexandra gave birth to her first child, a son who was given the name James. On 10 March, the Queen also gave birth to a son, her third – Prince Edward. Seven weeks later, on 28 April, a daughter, Helen, was born to the Duchess of Kent; while three days after that, on 1 May, Princess Margaret followed suit by giving birth to her only daughter, Sarah.

During what were to be the last four years of her life, family events, and those connected with her closest friends, continued to play a major part in Princess Marina's existence. In September 1964, for instance, she, her cousin Philip, Prince Charles and Princess Anne (who was to be one of the bridesmaids) flew to Athens to attend the celebrations marking the wedding of King Constantine of Greece to Princess Anne-Marie of Denmark, youngest daughter of King Frederick and Queen Ingrid.

Eighteen months later, in March 1966, Marina was accompanied to Amsterdam by Maow, Alexandra and Angus when she attended the marriage of Crown Princess Beatrix, the eldest of Queen Juliana's four daughters, to the handsome German diplomat, Claus von Amsberg. At the civil ceremony which preceded the religious rite, Alexandra acted as one of 'Trix's' witnesses; while outside in the cobbled streets – which little more than twenty years before had rung with the sound of goose-stepping Nazis – smoke bombs and riots forcefully reminded the bridegroom that he was both unpopular and unwelcome.

It was on this occasion that one member of the British royal party discovered that, while Princess Marina could be completely informal and easy-going, she was also a stickler for protocol. Lady Elizabeth Anson, a great-niece of the Queen Mother and at that time a girlfriend of Prince Michael, had been invited by Princess Beatrix to attend her as one of her bridesmaids. On the flight out to Amsterdam, Lady Elizabeth mentioned to Marina that the democratic Queen Juliana did not like being curtsied to. In the past, she explained, the Dutch Queen had always indicated that obeisance in the accepted form was unnecessary. Without hesitation Marina replied that, like it or not, curtsies would be made to Queen Juliana, adding that her party had all to remember that they represented Great Britain.

That March Princess Alexandra was five months pregnant with the fourth and last grandchild Marina was to know. On 31 July at Thatched House Lodge, the Ogilvys' twelve-bedroomed Georgian house in Richmond Park, the Princess gave birth to a daughter. A few weeks later, at her christening in the Chapel Royal at St James's Palace, the baby was named Marina in her grandmother's honour.

The following summer, the Duke and Duchess of Windsor visited London and, for the very first time, joined the royal family at a ceremony commemorating the centenary of Queen Mary's birth. Afterwards, as the rest of the royal family compulsively rushed off to Epsom for the Derby, Marina entertained the Windsors to lunch at Kensington Palace. It was the last time they were to meet but, in the same way that she had refused to join forces with the Queen Mother in ostracizing the Duke and Duchess, so Marina refused to poison her own children against them.

On 19 July 1968, for the first time in thirty-four years, Princess Marina was forced to cancel an official engagement. She had been due to visit the Frimley and Camberley Cadet Corps that afternoon but, because of a 'slight knee injury', had to ask Alexandra to deputize for her.

In a year that had opened quietly enough, Marina and Maow went on a private three-week safari to Kenya, Uganda and Tanzania. Later on that summer, the Princess planned to visit Olga and Paul at their home in Florence. As the months passed, however, Marina became increasingly troubled by her left leg. For no apparent reason it would suddenly give way and she would stumble or fall. Soon her left arm also grew weak. Marina invariably made light of it, and though she was only sixty-one, put it down to the approach of old age. 'We all grow old and we must face it,' she had said in a recent speech. 'For whatever our misfortunes have been, the disabilities and infirmities of old age are universal.' On 18 July she fell badly and was admitted to the National Hospital in London for tests. A day or two later, under instructions from her doctors to rest – and a nurse was engaged to make sure that she did – Marina went home. Although she was not to know, and Eddie, Alexandra and Michael kept it strictly to themselves, the results of the tests had revealed an inoperable brain tumour. According to her doctors' prognosis the Princess had, at the very most, no more than six or seven months to live.

On the day she returned from hospital Noël Coward took tea with Marina at Kensington Palace. 'She was in bed and looked very papery,' he wrote afterwards. 'I am worried about her. She was very cheerful, however, and we gossiped and giggled.' A month later, on Friday, 23 August, the Princess drove out to Richmond Park, where she spent two and a half hours sitting in the garden of Thatched House Lodge with Alexandra and the children. That Sunday – the twenty-sixth anniversary of Prince George's death – Alexandra and Angus joined Marina and Zoia Poklewska for lunch at Kensington Palace, and Zoia stayed on. The same night, the Princess had a blackout, and by nine o'clock the following morning she had drifted into an untroubled sleep. At 11.40 am on Tuesday 27 August, without having regained consciousness, Princess Marina died.

To her family who were with her at the end, the suddenness of Marina's death came as the most devastating shock. While they knew that it would happen some time within the next six months – a sufficiently shocking realization in itself – all was over in only five weeks.

In New York, where he heard the news, Cecil Beaton told a friend, 'She thought more about one and one's problems than seemed apparent. She had a formal manner but a conspiratorial gift for intimacy and in later years, I really felt she was a true friend.' In response to Beaton's message of sympathy, Princess

Alexandra wrote: 'Thank God my sweet Mama knew no pain or suffering. And now she is at peace.'

At about six o'clock on the evening of Thursday 29 August, the residents of Windsor Castle, who had been given notice to do so, drew their curtains. It must have seemed a strange order to have received on a long summer's evening, but at that hour the coffin of Prince George, Duke of Kent, beside which his widow had sat so often, was removed from the royal vault beneath the Albert Memorial Chapel. Solemnly placed in a hearse, it was driven up through the castle precincts and out through the private Home Park to the royal family's burial ground behind the Royal Mausoleum (tombhouse of Queen Victoria and the Prince Consort) at Frogmore. There, near the vast plane tree under which both the Duke and Duchess of Windsor would eventually be buried (in 1972 and 1986 respectively), two graves, side by side, had been freshly prepared. Into one of them Prince George's coffin was lowered.

Throughout the next morning, 30 August, royal friends and relations flew into Heathrow Airport. Among them were King Constantine and Queen Anne-Marie of the Hellenes, who arrived from Rome where they were now living in exile, and with them came 'Cousin Freddie', the Dowager Queen Frederika. Queen Helen of Romania flew in to attend her cousin's funeral; so too did Princess Paola of Liège, ex-King Umberto of Italy, and Prince Philip's sister, Princess Margarita of Hohenlohe-Langenberg. From his home in Paris came the Duke of Windsor, still trim enough to get into the morning suit he had worn at his wedding in 1937. Eddie was there to greet him.

While Heathrow was busy with its royal arrivals, a few miles away at Windsor Castle non-commissioned officers of The Queen's Regiment, the Devonshire and Dorset Regiment, and the Corps of Royal Electrical and Mechanical Engineers rehearsed carrying a dummy coffin down the west steps of St George's Chapel. Later that afternoon they would be responsible for carrying the body of their Colonel-in-Chief through the West Door and down those same uneven steps and, by then, their every move would have to be perfect. As the pall-bearers practised outside, the coffin of Princess Marina, Duchess of Kent, which had been brought to Windsor from Kensington Palace, lay within. Set on a catafalque between the tall, flickering candles Lord Stanhope had given to the chapel, the oak coffin lay in the silent, empty nave, draped with the Princess's personal standard which, in turn, had been partially draped with the blue and white Greek flag. On top lay two wreaths. The larger, made up of red, pink and yellow roses, was from Eddie, Alexandra and Michael. The smaller one, of blue and white flowers, was from Olga and Paul.

At 3 pm the funeral service began. The royal family followed the coffin into the quire, which glowed with heraldic emblems and the colourful banners of the Knights of the Garter, as from the organ loft the choristers sang the Sentences: 'I am the resurrection and the life.' The Queen and Prince Philip, the Queen Mother and the Duke of Windsor, followed by the rest of the royal family, were then conducted to their places in the second and third rows of the choir stalls. In front of them sat Princess Marina's immediate family, while on the opposite side of the black and white checkered aisle sat members of her household; Lady Rachel Pepys (formerly Lady Rachel Davidson) and Lady Balfour, her ladies-in-waiting; the Earl and Countess of Pembroke (formerly Lord and Lady Herbert); Sir Philip Hay, her private secretary; and Major Peter Clarke, now equerry to Princess Alexandra. Zoia Poklewska and Turia Campbell sat with them.

Psalm 23, 'The Lord is My Shepherd', was followed by the Lesson taken from the fourteenth chapter of the Gospel of St John, beginning, 'Let not your heart be troubled: ye believe in God, believe also in me.' The hymn *He Who Would Valiant Be* preceded the familiar funerary prayers, delivered by the Dean of Windsor and the Vicar of St Mary Abbots, and then the choir sang the collect hymn of the Holy Orthodox Church, *Give Rest, O Christ, to Thy Servant with Thy Saints*. As the service drew to a close one final hymn, *Lord of Our Life and God of Our Salvation*, was followed by the blessing delivered by the Archbishop of Canterbury, Dr Michael Ramsey, next to whom, an impressive figure in black robes and long grey beard, stood the Archimandrite Gregory Theodorus, Chancellor of the Diocese of Thyateira. Finally, as the mourners remained kneeling in silent prayer, the chapel was filled with the sound of the choristers, now singing the Anthem, *God Be in My Head*.

Moments later the royal procession reformed and, as they followed their mother's remains from the quire to the great West Door, the Duke of Kent, Princess Alexandra and Prince Michael held hands. Before stepping outside, however, in what was a sharp reminder of the royal family's training never to betray private feelings in public, they let go. At the top of the steps, looking on to the timbered fifteenth-century houses of the Horseshoe Cloisters, the family paused as the military pallbearers slowly carried the lead-lined coffin down to the waiting hearse. In news items around the world that was the only glimpse the public had of what had been a very private occasion. Within minutes the cortège had left for Frogmore, following the solitary route Prince George's coffin had taken only the night before.

When, in 1934, Princess Marina had first arrived in London as Prince George's fiancée, it will be recalled that men in the crowd outside Victoria Station had roared their approbation by shouting, 'Don't change – don't let them change you.' It was a mark of Marina's confidence in herself that the entreaties of her new admirers proved unnecessary. During her life as a member of the British royal family the monarchy as an institution may have begun to change, but Marina herself never did. In fact, if a study of her life reveals anything at all, it is surely that Marina was always determined to live according to her own beliefs and her own personal wishes.

At her memorial service, which the royal family attended, at Westminster Abbey on 25 October 1968 Dr Eric Abbott, then Dean of Westminster, commended Princess Marina for her 'spirit of spontaneity, her courage in adversity, her unswerving service to this land of her adoption [and] the mutual affection which was established between her and our people. . . .' What the Dean omitted to mention, through oversight or tact, was that with Princess Marina's death Britain had not only lost one of its most popular public figures but more espeicaly one of its last truly *royal* personalities.

Bibliography

Airlie, Mabell, Countess of, *Thatched with Gold*, Hutchinson 1962

Aronson, Theo, *Royal Family: Years of Transition*, John Murray 1983

Balfour, Neil, and Mackay, Sally, *Paul of Yugoslavia*, Hamish Hamilton 1980

Bloch, Michael, *The Duke of Windsor's War*, Weidenfeld & Nicolson 1982

Bryan, J., and Murphy, Charles J.V., *The Windsor Story*, Granada 1979

Buckle, Richard (ed.), *Self-Portrait with Friends: The Selected Diaries of Cecil Beaton 1926–74*, Weidenfeld & Nicolson 1979

Christopher of Greece, Prince, *Memoirs*, Hurst & Blackett 1938

Coward, Noël, *The Noël Coward Diaries*, Weidenfeld & Nicolson 1979

Duff, David, *Hessian Tapestry*, Frederick Muller 1967

Ellis, Jennifer, *The Duchess of Kent*, Odham Press 1952

Ellison, Grace, *The Life Story of Princess Marina*, Heinemann 1934

Fox, James, *White Mischief*, Penguin 1984

Rhodes James, Robert (ed.), *Chips: The Diaries of Sir Henry Channon*, Weidenfeld & Nicolson 1967

Kennett, Audrey and Victor, *The Palaces of Leningrad*, Thames & Hudson 1973

King, Stella, *Princess Marina: Her Life and Times*, Cassell 1969

Knightley, Philip, and Kennedy, Caroline, *An Affair of State*, Jonathan Cape 1987

Massie, Robert K., *Nicholas and Alexandra*, Victor Gollancz 1972

Mortimer, Penelope, *Queen Elizabeth: A Life of the Queen Mother*, Penguin 1987

Nicholas of Greece, Prince, *My Fifty Years*, Hutchinson 1926

Packard, Anne, HRH *The Duchess of Kent*, Pitkin 1950

Pope-Hennessey, James, *Queen Mary*, George Allen & Unwin 1959

Rose, Kenneth, *King George* v, *Weidenfeld & Nicolson 1983*

—*Kings, Queens and Courtiers*, Weidenfeld & Nicolson 1985

Thornton, Michael, *Royal Feud*, Pan 1985

Vickers, Hugo, *Cecil Beaton*, Weidenfeld & Nicolson 1985

Vogue, Royal Weddings 1922–81, Condé Nast 1981

Warwick, Christopher, *Princess Margaret*, Weidenfeld & Nicolson 1983

—*King George* VI *and Queen Elizabeth*, Sidgwick & Jackson, 1985

—Warwick, Christopher, *Abdication*, Sidgwick & Jackson 1986

Wentworth-Day, James, HRH *Princess Marina, Duchess of Kent*, Robert Hale 1962

Wheeler-Bennett, John W., *King George* VI, Macmillan 1958

Whiting, Audrey, *The Kents*, Hutchinson 1985

Windsor, The Duchess of, *The Heart Has its Reasons*, Michael Joseph 1956

Windsor, HRH The Duke of, *A King's Story*, Cassell 1951

Young, Kenneth (ed.), *The Diaries of Sir Robert Bruce-Lockhart 1915–1938*, Macmillan 1973

Newspapers and Periodicals: *Daily Express, Daily Mail, Daily Telegraph, Evening News, Evening Standard, Illustrated London News, Manchester Guardian*, Pitkin Pictorial booklets, *The Sphere, Sunday Dispatch, Sunday Express, The Sunday Times, The Times, Vogue.*

Index